In Response to the Steps

In Response to the Steps

Jan G.

Copyright © 2009 by Jan G.

ISBN:	Hardcover	978-1-4415-3257-2
Softcover	978-1-4415-3256-5

All rights reserved. Written permission must be secured from the publisher to use or reproduce any part of this book, except for brief quotations in critical reviews or articles.

Scripture quotations are taken from The New Revised Standard Version of the Bible. © 1989 by the Division of Christian Education of the National Council of the Churches of Christ in the U.S.A. All rights reserved.

The Twelve Steps and brief excerpts from the *Alcoholics Anonymous* and the *Twelve Steps and Twelve Traditions* are reprinted with permission of Alcoholics Anonymous World Services, Inc. ("AAWS") Permission to reprint brief excerpts from these books does not mean that AAWS has reviewed or approved the contents of this publication, or that AAWS necessarily agrees with the views expressed herein. A.A. is a program of recovery from alcoholism *only*—use of the Twelve Steps in connection with programs and activities which are patterned after A.A., but which address other problems, or in any other non-A.A. context, does not imply otherwise.

This book was printed in the United States of America.

To order additional copies of this book, contact:
Xlibris Corporation
1-888-795-4274
www.Xlibris.com
Orders@Xlibris.com

Contents

Introduction 7

Preface 11

1. Accepting Powerlessness 15
2. Finding hope 30
3. Making a Decision 37
4. Taking Inventory 45
5. Finding Freedom 56
6. Responding With a New Attitude 64
7. Embracing Humility 71
8. Preparing for Amends 78
9. Seeking forgiveness 84
10. Going Forward 91
11. Finding Power 97
12. Awakening Spiritually 103

Introduction

> LIFE IS DIFFICULT. THIS IS A GREAT TRUTH, ONE OF THE GREATEST TRUTHS. IT IS A GREAT TRUTH BECAUSE ONCE WE TRULY SEE THIS TRUTH, WE TRANSCEND IT. ONCE WE TRULY KNOW THAT LIFE IS DIFFICULT—ONCE WE TRULY UNDERSTAND AND ACCEPT IT—THEN LIFE IS NO LONGER DIFFICULT. BECAUSE ONCE IT IS ACCEPTED, THE FACT THAT LIFE IS DIFFICULT NO LONGER MATTERS.
>
> SCOTT PECK, *THE ROAD LESS TRAVELED*

It would be absolutely wonderful if we were born with the knowledge that life is difficult and that life will present challenges for all of us. Yet I have concluded through years of conversations with friends, colleagues, and professionals that life is not a journey that is pain free; rather it is a journey of choices and circumstances that present us with a mixture of joy and sadness, victory and defeat, hope and depression, questions and answers. Life is a gift that comes wrapped in mystery and simplicity. Often the mystery is unfolded in the simplicity if we are only able to be open to that strange phenomenon. I do not think that I was any different from most people in my youth and early adult years. I truly thought that there must be some way to create a life that would be wonderful and pain free—that I would find love and success and all of those "things" that I thought would make me happy and bring me a sense of personal worth.

Yet this was not my experience; rather, I embarked on a journey of discovery through personal pain that led me to a fascinating and amazing spiritual transformation. This transformation came through my discovery of who I was created to be and my commitment to follow age-old spiritual truths. I had struggled to find a way to identify and accept my own reality, having always thought that I should be something other than what I was. If you asked me, "Who are you?" I would have given a typical response with titles such as computer consultant, manager, parent, daughter, or sports nut. I had no idea of who I was as a person.

The discovery of my "personhood" came as a result of living my life based on the Twelve Steps that have been made famous through the fellowship of Alcoholics Anonymous. I have come to understand that these principles are a collection of wisdom that has been present to mankind throughout the ages. This wisdom took the form of the Twelve Steps in the twentieth century and became available to the general public after the publication of the book *Alcoholics Anonymous* in 1939.

I believe that God had been trying to communicate these profound truths over the millennia in many different ways. The book of Exodus records an event in the life of Moses where God reveals Himself as "I am who I am," and He asks Moses to share this news with his people so they would know that there is one, and only one, God. And so Moses did this as he led the Israelites out of slavery in Egypt—an event that became the touchstone of Israel's relationship with God. And then when the Israelites struggled in this relationship, God gave Moses the Ten Commandments as guidelines to help them understand how to live a life that would bring them peace and joy. Over time, the people managed to convert these ten simple commandments into more than six hundred laws. God then decided that He would appear in person to help get his people back on track with what is really important, and to try to simplify it for them; so he sent His Son Jesus Christ to share the Good News with them. Jesus taught his followers that:

> "'You shall love the Lord your God with all your heart, and with all your soul, and with all your mind.' This is the greatest and first commandment. And a second is like it: 'You shall love your neighbor as yourself.' On these two commandments hang all the law and the prophets." (Matthew 22:37-40)

The outcome of this simplification of God's plan to help us live life to the fullest resulted in the church's bickering over interpretations of Christ's proclamation of the gospel, and so there were more than nineteen hundred denominations of the Christian religion by the year 1900. By 2000 there were more than 33,800![1] So in 1935 God once again chose to reveal Himself to just one man—a man who had struggled for years with the disease of alcoholism: Bill Wilson. He helped Bill to get sober and to share his sobriety with one other man, Dr. Bob Smith. These two men then shared their experience with others, and this small group of recovering alcoholics came to realize that they had engaged in a certain process that had kept them sober. They finally recorded their experience and this process and called it the Twelve Steps. God inspired them as he had inspired others in the past with His truth. The difference this time was that God sent this inspiration in simple language that was put into a simple order. He numbered his directions from one to twelve, and then inspired this group of recovering alcoholics to preserve this treasure of truth by forming an organization that had no leadership fight over power and prestige. He helped them to understand that anonymity would preserve their success. No more organized religion; no more ordained or elected leaders.

Much of the spiritual wisdom of great theologians and philosophers has been simplified into these Twelve Steps. As a result of following these steps and making them part of my life, my life has been filled with joy. It is not a life without pain or disappointment. It is not a life without struggles. Rather, it is one that honors who I was created to be—a pilgrim on a journey that is centered in a relationship with my Higher Power, whom I have recognized as God. This is a relationship that enables me to be at peace with who I am, and to be in right relationship with those people in my life whom I encounter on a regular basis. This is an amazing concept that I could not have imagined in my youth.

This book is intended to inspire others to share in this twelve-step journey. I believe that I was fortunate to have what is often referred to as "the gift of desperation" that enabled me to make a commitment to follow this path. But I also believe that this path is available to any who choose to follow it. History has now shown us that over the past seventy years, since the gift of this wisdom was given to this small band of recovering alcoholics, these steps work for any individual who chooses to incorporate them in their life. These steps have been adopted by families of alcoholics (Alanon), gamblers (Gamblers Anonymous), overeaters (Overeaters Anonymous), drug addicts (Narcotics Anonymous), and many others.

The beauty of the steps is that they work for everyone because we are all spiritual in nature, even if we are not necessarily associated with any particular religion or philosophy. Also, we don't need to have an addiction in order to follow the steps. The Twelve Steps are simple to understand, but require commitment, discipline, and perseverance if we choose to live by them as a way of life. There is a mystery in the simplicity of the steps, and that mystery is that if you choose to live by their principles—use this path as a way of life—the virtues in the steps will develop in your life through your own experience. You don't need to have these virtues to begin this journey—you only need the willingness to begin. My hope is that this reflection of one pilgrim's experiences and insights will open the door of willingness for many!

Preface

These reflections are written in a parallel fashion to the Twelve Steps of Alcoholics Anonymous. Each step is addressed in an individual chapter. The first section of each chapter begins with the text of one of the steps, followed by my personal reflections on my experience in coming to understand the meaning of the step in my own recovery.

The next section offers insight into the use of the step by those who are not recovering from alcoholism. I believe that the steps are applicable to all people who seek spiritual growth, and therefore, the second section in each chapter is titled "Step One (Two, etc.) for Everyone." The primary premise of the book is that all of us are powerless over many things in our lives, some of which are addictive and result in behavior that is similar to alcoholic behavior. This section of the chapter contains information that is useful to any who are seeking spiritual growth.

The steps are simple, but are not necessarily easy to integrate into our lives. There is often mystery involved in coming to understand this simplicity because it often contradicts the understanding of life as viewed through our culture. Who would ever think that you "need to surrender to win"? This type of philosophy is unraveled in the final section of the chapter and it is introduced with the subtitle "The Mystery Revealed in the Simplicity of Step ____."

The final portion of each chapter contains a list of self study questions that can be used to assist the reader in incorporating the step in his or her life. These questions can also be used for a group discussion of the step and the group members' experiences in trying to live by the steps.

The flow of the steps provides a profound and infallible progression of spiritual growth. The first three steps begin by helping us establish a firm foundation with the God of our own understanding. Based in this foundation, steps four through seven enable us to look at who we really are and to grow in this knowledge of self. This exploration can only be truly successful when we have the sure knowledge that we are loved by our Creator. This solid relationship with God and self then enables us to focus our attention on our relationships with others. This happens in steps eight and nine. The remainder of the steps provide guidance in how to maintain this newfound way of life.

The following are the chapter titles followed by the text of the associated step from the Twelve Steps of Alcoholics Anonymous:

Chapter 1. Accepting Powerlessness

> We admitted we were powerless over alcohol—that our lives had become unmanageable.

Chapter 2. Finding Hope

> Came to believe that a Power greater than ourselves could restore us to sanity.

Chapter 3. Making a Decision

> Made a decision to turn our will and our lives over to the care of God *as we understood Him*.

Chapter 4 Taking Inventory

> Made a searching and fearless moral inventory of ourselves.

Chapter 5. Finding Freedom

> Admitted to God, to ourselves, and to another human being the exact nature of our wrongs.

Chapter 6. Responding with a New Attitude

> Were entirely ready to have God remove all these defects of character.

Chapter 7. Embracing Humility

> Humbly asked Him to remove our shortcomings.

Chapter 8. Preparing for Amends

> Made a list of all persons we had harmed, and became willing to make amends to them all.

Chapter 9. Seeking Forgiveness

> Made direct amends to such people wherever possible, except when to do so would injure them or others.

Chapter 10. Going Forward

> Continued to take personal inventory and when we were wrong promptly admitted it.

Chapter 11. Finding Power

> Sought through prayer and meditation to improve our conscious contact with God, *as we understood Him,* praying only for knowledge of His will for us and the power to carry that out.

Chapter 12. Awakening Spiritually

> Having had a spiritual awakening as the result of these Steps, we tried to carry this message to alcoholics, and to practice these principles in all our affairs.

Chapter 1

ACCEPTING POWERLESSNESS

STEP ONE

**WE ADMITTED WE WERE POWERLESS OVER ALCOHOL—
THAT OUR LIVES HAD BECOME UNMANAGEABLE.**

We are all powerless. This is a universal truth about our human condition. Yet, one of our greatest problems as human beings is our egocentric belief that we have total control over the events and circumstances in our lives. We are held hostage to the concepts that if we try hard enough, if we believe deeply enough, and if we work long enough, we will be able to control our own destinies. I am a proponent of hard work, diligence, and discipline; I know that these virtues are certainly necessary to accomplish many goals in our lives, such as education, the development of sports or musical talents, and even behavioral changes suggested through therapy. When it comes to our spiritual lives, though, these virtues alone can't free us from our bondage to an addiction or help us to grow into a deep relationship with our creator. However, they can become "tools" that will assist us in our journey. Step One, therefore, takes the form of a universal truth when we acknowledge our powerlessness over any substance, person, or relationship in our life. The remainder of the Twelve Steps can lead us back to a position of power after significant practice with the spiritual principles of the steps. This power will be something that is given to us after we are rooted in this new way of life.

Jan G.

The good news is that any person who engages in the principles of the steps can experience this amazing power in his or her daily life.

Another spiritual truth that is intrinsic to Step One is this: if we are still operating under the delusion that our greatest power comes from within ourselves and is based on our own talents, capabilities, and skills, then we will have a life that has become unmanageable in some significant way. For the alcoholic, this unmanageability will express itself in repeated episodes of trouble as a result of drinking alcohol. For the drug addict, there will be problems from using drugs, and for the overeater there will be difficulty with weight. The most deceptive symptoms of unmanageability will perhaps come in the guise of situations that our culture promotes, such as working long hours to the point of sacrificing family relationships or good mental or physical health. Doctors, lawyers, and executives are not the only people who fall victim to this excess; many who are seeking to climb the corporate ladder or own their own small businesses also succumb to this unmanageable life style. We call these people "workaholics." Marriages, families, and close relationships are often torn apart because of this pattern of behavior. Eventually workaholics begin to lose themselves in the process. Excessive exercising or playing sports can also have the negative effect of eliminating other important things in life. Though exercise and sports are healthy activities, when we engage in them to the extent that we start to forget about school, family, and friends, this good practice can be classified as living a life that is unmanageable.

When I approached the Twelve Steps for the first time, I had no concept of powerlessness or unmanageability. In fact, I took pride in just the opposite. I relished the fact that one of my greatest skills was in the ability to be a leader and to organize and manage anything—large scale computer projects, my household, parties, or sorority events. You name it and I was ready to do it! I had acquired a significant number of "things" and accomplishments: I had two college degrees, one of which was a Masters in Business Administration where I had graduated cum laude. I had a good paying job, owned a share of a house, drove a nice car, and had many friends. I had been president of my sorority in college and had achieved some small goals as an athlete in high school and college. My resume looked good, and my outward presentation was not bad looking either; I dressed nicely and talked with conviction.

Yet, with hindsight, I can now describe the true reality at that time in my life. I was a person filled with fear and despair. I was unable to live alone, was terrified of driving over bridges, was afraid of the dark, and worst of all, was afraid of myself! I did not know or understand how to "live" life. I was seeking a meaningful relationship with another person, yet was unable to have a meaningful relationship with myself. I was terrified that others would reject me if they ever knew who I was on the inside. I spent a large amount of time trying to accomplish goals and win trophies so that I could earn my way into some kind of indescribable acceptance. I thought that if I moved up a career ladder in my chosen profession I would be happy. I was desperately trying to find happiness and was looking every place outside of myself to find it. I believed if I could find and acquire this undefined and elusive "it," I would then feel good and find the happiness I wanted.

Alcohol played a large part in my life at this time, since I felt alcohol would guarantee that I "be like everyone else." I thought that all people who drank were having fun, and those who did not drink were basically leading boring lives. I acquired this idea from watching television as a kid. I was enamored with the television show "77 Sunset Strip" starring Efrem Zimbalist, Jr., and was very aware of scotch and a cigarette as part of his character's regular facade. I attributed his smiling face and happiness on the show to these vices that were missing from my home environment. As a teenager, I could think of nothing else that I saw on the show that I could identify as missing from my life. My parents didn't drink or smoke—and therefore I concluded that it must be alcohol that made the difference. So I went off to college in 1965, and within a year I had found people who wanted to party. I was having fun when I started to drink and smoke, so I set aside the concept that any kind of spiritual path would bring the joy that I was seeking.

The partying and fun did not last for long. By 1976 I had reached a point of desperation in my life. I was having trouble with my drinking, but even more trouble with living in my own skin. A dear friend of mine was brave enough to confront me about my drinking behavior and told me how I could get some help. I had this information for awhile before I was ready to take any action. Finally, I had a car accident where I totaled my car and was inches away from causing serious physical harm to myself and my roommate, who was in the car with me. The desperation that I felt helped me to finally become willing to ask for help and to listen to others. I picked up the telephone, called the self-help group that my friend had suggested that I contact, and was introduced to people who were living their lives based on the Twelve Steps of Alcoholics Anonymous. I had no reason to believe that talking with these people would provide me with any answers, but my desperation opened a door of willingness to at least try. As I listened to people discuss the first step, where I needed to admit to powerlessness and unmanageability, I was very frustrated. Though I desperately wanted to be able to stop the trouble in my life, I did not understand how anything about this step, particularly accepting my powerlessness, would be able to help me. I knew there was a relationship between the trouble in my life and my drinking, but I could not understand how I was powerless over alcohol. This concept made no sense to me. I believed that I was in control of my drinking, and that I needed help in learning how to control it.

There was another immediate complication for me with my introduction to this group of people and the Twelve Steps that they adopted as a solution to their drinking problem. I saw the Twelve Steps and had no way to comprehend what they meant or how they applied to my life. So I tried to listen to other things that they were saying. I was trying to find something that I could understand that would be helpful. One of the first things they made sure I heard was that they no longer drank any alcohol. They drank nothing that contained alcohol: no beer, no wine, no hard liquor. They told me that if I really wanted to keep away from trouble, I would have to stop drinking. Fortunately, they suggested that I try to do this for just one day—not the rest of my life. They asked me if I blacked out when I drank. I had no idea of what they were talking about, so they rephrased the question and asked if I lost memory of what I had been doing when I was drinking. I said yes and had to admit that I, in fact, was a blackout drinker.

It was encouraging to talk to these people; they were there to listen and to help. Then they suggested that I start each day by getting on my knees and asking for help from some power greater than myself to stay away from one drink for that day. I had no idea what that meant and was terrified that if I did what was suggested, God would speak out loud to me! But I did it anyway by closing the door to my bedroom, getting down on my knees, putting a pillow over my head so I could not be seen, and then asking for help to stay away from one drink for that day. It worked, and I did *not* hear a voice; so I did it the next day, and the next, and soon it became a habit.

Then my new friends told me to get down on my knees at night and thank that power for giving me the ability to not pick up a drink that day. I took their suggestions and was able to do what they said only because of the fear that was inside me. I was terrified that if I drank again, I would go into an alcoholic blackout, drive my car, kill myself, or worse than that, kill someone else. I later came to find out that the power that was greater than me, whom I came to call God, did not really care about *how* I did the things to help me not pick up a drink and to stay sober. The details of my actions were not important; it was my honesty and willingness to do whatever actions I took to the best of my ability. God honors my willingness and my efforts, as long as I am trying to do any of these steps to the best of my ability, even though I will never be able to work the steps to perfection.

I also came to find out that this phrase—to the best of my ability—was a very important concept. I could not compare my progress or my results to any other person's program. This concept was critical for me to understand because I had always compared myself to others in academics in school, in sports, and in my job. Avoiding this kind of comparison was a new idea for me to grasp.

In Response to the Steps

As I was able to stay away from drinking for a few weeks, I started being able to think more clearly. I remember being aware of the thought that perhaps I would be able to stop drinking for awhile, but had no hope that my life would improve beyond that one change. Fear, though, of what might happen if I were to drink again, enabled me to continue to listen to what these people had to say. Over time, I was able to understand some rather profound truths about myself and about life in general. It took about six months of listening to many people share many stories before I was able to *identify* with what they were saying instead of trying to *compare* myself to them. Initially I was able to keep from drinking because of fear, but in a short amount of time I was able to engage in the steps on my own because I wanted to be sober. This ability to identify and not compare was a miracle, and it happened as a result of my trying to understand Step One and admit that I was powerless over alcohol and that my life was unmanageable.

Another important lesson during my early sobriety was that I did not have to "accept" that I was powerless over alcohol, I only needed to "admit" I was powerless over alcohol. This meant that I did not have to understand why or how I was powerless. I did not have to like the fact that I could not drink without getting into trouble. I just had to make an admission that I was powerless—that I had no power over how much I would drink or when I would be able to stop drinking once I started. This gave me some comfort because I truly did not understand how I was powerless over alcohol or anything else in my life. But I did understand that I did not have the power to stop myself from drinking too much. If I had that power, I would have used it. I knew that I didn't want to have trouble with my drinking. I wanted to be able to just have a good time, but I was not able to do that any longer. I was able to "admit" that this control was gone.

There was a very helpful tool that gave me further understanding my own powerlessness over alcohol. People suggested that I try to write a list of all of the things that I could remember that caused harm to myself or others, embarrassing situations, blackout drinking, and any other items that I associated with trouble as a result of drinking. This list was called a Step One inventory. Then, I learned over time to also focus on what alcohol did to me on the inside, where my disease lives. Alcoholism is not defined by what you drink, who you drink with, or how much you drink. This disease is defined by what happens to you *when* you drink. My mentor helped me to understand this by looking at the inventory of both my behavior and my feelings. It was important to look at the outside trouble that I had when drinking, but if I only focused on the outside things that surrounded my drinking, then I would always be able to find someone who had worse things happen to them than I had experienced.

Jan G.

These new friends of mine told me that the disease of alcoholism is threefold—physical, mental, and spiritual. I was amazed to find out that this made sense to me. After not drinking for awhile, I was able to be honest with myself and see how this was true in my life. Certainly, the physical results of drinking were easy to identify: drunken behavior, the inability to stop drinking after I had started, and outside problems such as car accidents. But I also came to realize that drinking was part of what had been causing my decay on the inside, that somehow alcoholism was directly linked to my fears, despair, and self-loathing. Some of these feelings came as a direct result of my internal reactions to the outside problems. But this disease also fed the negative feelings as a result of my inability to have a spiritual dimension in my life. We are all spiritual beings—and this is not in reference to anything religious. It means that part of me is spirit, and this part of me needs to be in a relationship with the spiritual realm of this world. When this truth is not recognized and pursued, then we become spiritually bankrupt and try to live life by assuming that we have control over people, places, and things. If I am not in a relationship with my spiritual world where I acknowledge that there is something bigger than me that is in charge my life, then my mind convinces me that I need to be in control. I take over and create havoc in the lives around me. I was bankrupt spiritually—and had been for a long time.

It was only when I started looking at the "inside" mental and spiritual events and taking this part of my inventory, that I was able to finally identify with others who were sharing their stories. When I started to listen to folks talk about remorse, I realized that I had remorse too—for things that I said and did after drinking. When others talked about their fear, loneliness, and despair, I was relieved to learn that I was not the only one who had ever felt that way! When people talked about feeling lonely in a room full of people, I knew I had felt that too. Depression, self loathing—all of these emotions were part of their disease, and mine, as well. And so, when they told me that these feelings and thoughts had gone away after they stopped drinking, I came to believe if it was true for them, maybe it could be true for me.

So, what about this powerlessness?

After some months of listening and learning, I heard the simplicity of powerlessness described in a way that made sense to me. People told me that when they took one drink, they could not predict the outcome of that event. They could not predict if they were going to take only one drink, drink until they passed out, drink until they embarrassed themselves, or drink until they got into some kind of trouble. *They said that every time they drank, they did not get into trouble. But every time they experienced trouble, they had been drinking!* How simple! The mystery was gone, and I had a glimpse of what powerlessness meant. This unpredictability and honest appraisal of the cause of my troubles was something that I could understand and relate to. I heard it said that a man takes a drink, then the drink takes a drink, and then the drink takes the man. At first I thought a lot of these sayings were trite, but I soon came to treasure them. They were simple statements that even a confused person like me could understand. I was finally on my way to understanding and accepting my own powerlessness over alcohol. I was able to acknowledge that I could not predict what would happen if I picked up a drink. I could not predict if I would have a black out when I drank, and I could not even predict if I would be able to physically make it to a car to drive while in a blackout. If I drank, worse things could happen to me before I ever got into a car. I concluded that I should simply not spend the energy trying to figure out what would happen if I picked up one drink. It made much more sense to focus on what would happen if I didn't pick up a drink at all and to work on these Twelve Steps as a way of life.

This ability to admit to my powerlessness over alcohol enabled me to address my disease on an intellectual level. But in order to progress with the steps on a deeper level, I needed to move that information from my head to my heart. I needed to take the facts that I was able to articulate, and move to a place of acceptance of my powerlessness.

I began to engage in a process that I really wasn't conscious of at the time, but something that I came to understand with hindsight.

It has to do with the nature of acceptance of powerlessness and how it happens to us. Arriving at a level of acceptance of any situation or attribute is really a process. Sometimes we move quickly through that process and other times we move slowly. This insight came from reading Elisabeth Kubler-Ross's book *On Death and Dying*. It might seem odd that the topic of death can be related to the concept of powerlessness, but after going through the experience and reflecting on it, it makes sense. In order to accept truth, our old idea needs to go away, change, and in a sense die. The five emotional stages of dying that Kubler-Ross introduces are: denial, anger, bargaining, depression, and acceptance. This, in fact, is the process that is used to come to any level of acceptance in any situation.

For me, my denial took the form of my believing that I was not an alcoholic, and I did not have a problem with alcohol My denial survived with thoughts such as "I am too young to be an alcoholic. I still have a job. I am not homeless, or drunk all of the time." My denial was the part of me that wanted to compare myself to those who had worse troubles than my own. In order to get past the denial, I had to learn to identify with the people who were sharing their experience with me. My denial was broken when I no longer compared my differences with them, but instead was able to see and embrace my similarities with those who had self-identified as alcoholics and were staying sober by not drinking.

The anger came in the form of "why me?" Why was I an alcoholic? Why couldn't I drink like others who didn't have a problem with alcohol? Why did I have to stop drinking so early in life, when others were able to drink until they were much older? I was told to not ask why, rather to ask "Why not?" Why not me? Why was I so special that this malady could not have affected me? It was a waste of time to ask "why me?" and after realizing this, I was able to move on to the bargaining stage.

For me, the bargaining stage didn't last long, because something inside of me realized that I really did not have control over alcohol when I drank. My progression with the disease had been rapid, and blackout drinking was always part of my story over the ten years that I drank. But I heard other stories of people who tried to bargain with their disease by trying to manipulate and control their drinking. They tried to switch from the "hard stuff"—whiskey, vodka, scotch, or whatever—and only drink beer or wine. Somehow, our culture had identified alcoholics with drunks who only drank a bottle of whiskey out of a brown bag! This is obviously not true. Others tried to drink only on weekends as a reward for being "good" during the week. Others spoke of experiences where they were in a jam and prayed to God for help and promised never to drink again, only to find themselves after some amount of time in another jam because they did pick up the drink and eventually ended up back at the same place or worse than they had been before.

I saw this reality happen when I first got sober. I met a woman who had been sober for twenty-five years. She had been homeless and lived on the streets of Boston when she first stopped drinking. With sobriety, she was able to enter into a new way of life, and married a man in the program. After he died in her twenty-sixth year of sobriety, she began drinking and ended up dying on the streets as a homeless drunk. I learned from this sad situation that the disease of alcoholism will never be cured in an individual. There is no way ever to drink in safety—and there is no bargaining, or will power, or control that will change the nature of the disease and one's ability to drink without problems.

When I understood that there was no way to drink in safety, or to bargain for a solution to my drinking problems, the next stage, depression, came. I felt depressed that I had lost the one part of my life that I thought was going to allow me to fit in with the world. I was depressed that I would appear to those who were able to drink in safety as a wimp, or a "Goody Two-Shoes" (whatever that meant!). But eventually I was able to see that most of the world does not drink as my friends and I did. It was only because I surrounded myself with people who drank like me that I had that perception. I found out that alcohol was not a friend that I was losing; rather it was an enemy that I was choosing to leave behind and remove from my life.

And finally, the acceptance came to me. At first, it was only a glimpse and would last for a short time, but then it grew and became part of my conscious thoughts. The stages of Kubler-Ross's death and dying are not sequential and experienced only once. They repeat themselves and occur often in a random order. But eventually, the process results in acceptance if one is persistent. The facts that I had identified in my first-step inventory, and the knowledge that I could no longer drink in safety moved from my head to my heart.

It is important to note that because we arrive at this level of acceptance of powerlessness does not mean that it is permanent. Another one of the phrases that I heard early in my sobriety was that "eternal vigilance was the price of sobriety." If I was not vigilant in my contact with these folks who had experience in the Twelve Steps, and if I did not persist in my pursuit of the steps as a way of life, there was an excellent chance that I would drink again.

The second part of this step requires us to admit that life has become unmanageable. Unmanageability is a cousin to powerlessness and often accompanies the gift of desperation. This unmanageability is directly related to the object of our powerlessness. For alcoholics, the disease causes havoc both internally and externally. The disease creates internal unmanageability that is in direct response to the outward situations that we can no longer control. In extreme cases, there are stories of alcoholics who drive drunk and have accidents, perhaps resulting in the loss of life. There can be family problems, job performance problems, or health related problems. The alcoholic who makes promises that things will be different the next time, and finds that this control is not possible over the long haul, will deal with shame, guilt, and anger that many times turn to self-hatred and depression. Loneliness, anxiety, despair, and fear are also common companions to the one suffering from addiction. Life can definitely be unmanageable because there is no longer any control that seems to work to prevent the next episode of trouble.

I had the job title of manager, so this was another struggle for me. My title and my job description required me to manage projects and people. And since I was still somewhat successful in those endeavors, it seemed illogical that my life was unmanageable. Again, I listened to others and their experience.

It is not easy to separate the two concepts of powerlessness and unmanageability when dealing with the disease of alcoholism. Initially I had focused on my powerlessness during most of my time of trying to stay sober, and the idea of unmanageability kind of slid off my tongue as an afterthought to the word *powerless*. Yet I was told that the step was not complete until I could identify how my powerlessness had affected the manageability of my life. I turned to my mentor, and with her help and others, was able to examine this issue with greater care. I saw that my job performance had slipped as a result of extended lunches and lack of energy after late nights—regardless of the amount of sleep I had. I realized that I was not taking care of myself physically, even though I continued to play sports. I didn't have a healthy diet or a program of exercise. And

Jan G.

I was consistently making social decisions based upon the presence or absence of alcohol; I really had no time for mingling with people who did not drink. I tolerated these situations while waiting for an opportunity to find some way to go someplace where there was alcohol. And once again, there was no evidence of spiritual discipline in my life. Alcohol was managing me; I was not managing my life. It was controlling where I went and who I spent time with. This brief inventory, along with the inventory of how I was powerless over alcohol, was sufficient to help me understand the depth of the disease running rampant in my life. I was finally able to see my need to admit that I was powerless and that my life had become unmanageable.

We can relapse into the old insanity if we are not vigilant in pursuing sobriety. The body, mind, and spirit are the hosts of the disease of alcoholism, not the bottle, can, or keg. If we don't continue with the steps as a way of life, then the disease can take control and the denial can return. But if we choose to live by the principles that are contained in these steps, then we can experience a life as described by a dear friend in recovery—an extraordinary ordinary life! Step One is the foundation for the other eleven steps. Without a clear understanding and acceptance of this step, it will be more difficult to experience the best of what the other steps have to offer.

STEP ONE FOR EVERYONE

The Twelve Steps are applicable to all of life for anyone who desires to live by them. It seems that the difficulty for most people is to find the motivation to take them seriously and to put forth the commitment and perseverance they require. For alcoholics and anyone else dealing with an addiction or compulsive behavior this type of program is compelling because these individuals come to it after experiencing some extreme difficulty and are desperate for help. But the steps are not limited to those who have experienced some tragedy or trauma in their life. They are spiritual axioms that are applicable to all people regardless of their life experience or religious beliefs.

The first step is usually the step that turns people away if they do not recognize that they have a problem with some addictive behavior. However, we all make decisions every day that impact what happens to us and to those around us, but in the end, the outcome is out of our control and we are truly powerless over the outcome. We can study to be a doctor or teacher, but what happens if we experience a serious disease or accident that limits our physical ability to achieve our goal? We can parent our children with the best skills available to us, yet science tells us that all of us have a specific and unique genetic makeup that determines much of who we are; therefore if a parent wants a child to be a concert pianist and the child does not have the aptitude for this profession, then all of the training and education in the world will not create an accomplished pianist. It is a fallacy to think that anyone has power over any person, place, or situation in their life. The truth of the matter is that we are indeed powerless over outcomes of our actions.

Try replacing the word *alcohol* in the first step and tailor it to any addiction or troubling condition in your life. It can read, "We admitted that we were powerless over (food, drugs, gambling, my spouse, my son or daughter, my parents, my job or whatever) and our lives had become unmanageable." Or the two words "over alcohol" can be eliminated and the step can read simply as, "We admitted we were powerless and our lives had become unmanageable." Either approach is valid in order to adapt the step to any life situation. Ultimately I came to understand the step for many aspects of my own life. I have been able to use it for specific situations such as smoking and being powerless over cigarettes and for compulsive eating. I was also fortunate to be able to use is it in the generic sense when applying it to my relationship with God and my spiritual journey. I truly am powerless, and am grateful that I have come to that understanding.

The process of acceptance is also applicable to all situations in our lives. The Kubler-Ross stages of death and dying apply to any major change in our life that requires acknowledgement of powerlessness and unmanageability, and ultimately acceptance of these conditions. The stages can apply to loss of job, loved one, marriage, or simply leaving a home where you have lived for many years.

The denial, anger, bargaining, and depression tend to cycle back and forth, sometimes in a random order. But when we work through all stages, then we arrive at a point of acceptance. Now understand that acceptance does not generate joy or happiness. It is not a state of euphoria. Nor is it to be confused with defeat. Rather, it is more a sense of relief when the struggle is gone and replaced with a quiet sense of peace and resolution. Acceptance is what opens the door to hope. Hope for freedom from whatever situation was rendering us powerless.

Once I acquired knowledge of this process and its characteristics, I then came to see it in many different areas of my life. It was certainly true for my acceptance of my alcoholic drinking, but it was also true when I was trying to face the truth that my marriage was over, that I had no power over my children, my smoking addiction, my eating disorder, and my sexual orientation. Each of these areas of my life required me to move through these five stages of death and dying. And for each of these situations, I needed guidance from others who had gone before me and walked the path that I had to walk. It always began with denial and finally ended with acceptance. Some people I know have chosen to remain in the denial phase for critical situations in their life, and have consequently remained entrenched in their powerlessness with little hope for change. The reality is that they will not experience change without first accepting their powerlessness. The evidence is in the fact that they still try to control their behavior, a person, a place or a thing that is causing them pain.

It does not matter if you understand this process of stages resulting in acceptance. But you do have to experience its five stages—there are no shortcuts to acceptance. This happens faster for some people than for others, and certainly, for those who get stuck in the denial stage, it will never happen. People with the diseases of alcoholism or drug addiction will ultimately die from the disease if they are not able to pass through the denial stage and begin to work on the other stages moving to acceptance. Others who do not engage in the process to the fullest will end up with bitter resentment over a broken relationship, a life of sorrow over the death of a loved one, or simply trying to change people or events in their life that are impossible to influence. This is especially true for those who are family and friends of people who have one of the addiction diseases. They too have to engage in the stages of acceptance and then ultimately work the remaining steps in their life if they hope to achieve any peace or serenity within their situation.

There can be a false hope that encourages denial, where we believe that life will be better one day—all will be well when something happens to make the nightmare go away. The problem is that the nightmare will not go away until we accept our powerlessness, and take steps to restore ourselves to health. Otherwise, if we choose not to confront our problem, the unmanageability will continue to bring discomfort, despair, and ultimately tragedy. But we can intervene and stop the progression by living by the Twelve Steps.

One last point on the process of acceptance of being powerless is that this acceptance does not eliminate my responsibility for action. Just because I am powerless over alcohol does not mean that I need to take no action in assuring that I will not drink for one day at a time. Because I am powerless over my children does not mean that I am no longer responsible for exercising good parenting skills in raising them. Because I am powerless over my food consumption, or my sexual preference does not eliminate the need to find solutions to my given situations. I am responsible for my actions, but I cannot predict the outcome of my actions.

> Powerlessness means that I cannot predict the outcome of my own behavior. It also means that I am out of control if I need to control my behavior around any substance or circumstance that is causing me problems.

Powerlessness means that I cannot predict the outcome of my own behavior. It also means that I cannot control my behavior around any substance or circumstance that is causing me problems. People who do not have a drinking problem don't have to stop and think about how to make sure that they don't go over a certain limit. Usually they don't even desire to have an amount of alcohol that would cause

In Response to the Steps

a problem. I remember being shocked when I discovered that there were really people who only wanted one drink—and might not even finish that one drink.

The addiction lies to us when the mind says, "I will feel better if I . . ." I will feel better if I have a drink, or eat, or spend money, or win some money. Or the addiction will lie by saying, "Well, maybe I do have a problem with my drinking (gambling, eating, or whatever), but I am not as bad as John (or Sue, or Joe, or Harry). When I get that bad, I will do something about this situation." And then when we get that bad, we find someone else who is having more trouble than we are. Someone who drinks more, weighs more, gambles more, or spends more. And another lie can be "Well, I will take care of this problem drinking, gambling, spending, eating, or whatever tomorrow." The problem with this lie is that tomorrow never comes, we only have today!

Once we acquire an addiction or a compulsion, we need to recognize the problem and do something about it. It will not go away, and it will not get better unless we as admit the truth and choose to get help in dealing with it. To *admit* means to *enter into*. We have a ticket that admits us into an event like a movie, show, or sporting event. Admitting to powerlessness allows us to enter into a new way of life, a new found freedom, a path of recovery, a journey to find hope, joy, peace, and serenity. But all of this takes time. When I first engaged in these steps, I was told that at the beginning *time* would mean *this I must endure*, but ultimately, it would lead me to a period in my life where *time* would mean *this I must enjoy*. These simple phrases helped me to stay committed to this process when life became difficult, and the effort that I needed to put forth appeared impossible and at best overwhelming.

But most of all, I needed to find people who understood these steps so that I could engage in them with others who could share their experience with me. I would have never been able to pursue these steps and stay focused if I had not had people to help interpret them to me. It is not a journey that can be traveled alone. It is not a process that can be studied and expected to produce results in an academic manner. It cannot be managed like a work project with a project plan. The steps are meant to become a way of life, and they work for everyone. But everyone must discover their own path with the help of others along the way.

THE MYSTERY REVEALED IN THE SIMPLICITY OF STEP ONE

> Asking for help is a sign of strength, not of weakness.
>
> *Quote from Dressbarn (Women's Clothing Store)*

Part of the power and the beauty of the Twelve Steps is that we do not do them with perfection, so we are not expected to grasp this concept of powerlessness and unmanageability before moving onto the other steps. I have discovered from others" experience, and now from my own experience, that the most important ingredient in this process is one's willingness to try. *Success is found in the effort, and the mystery is found in this simple act of obedience. Through obedience we enter into the new way of life by admitting our powerlessness and our unmanageability.* This admission is the beginning of the process towards acceptance. God honors our efforts and our desire to work the steps. Our success is measured in not drinking, or not engaging in a destructive behavior that we are trying to overcome. Our success is measured by our willingness to grow spiritually and by engaging in an intentional process to achieve that growth. The mystery that is revealed is simply that these steps do not follow the standards for measuring success that we encounter in the world. The first time a person asks for help is the beginning of admitting that he or she is powerless. The success of Step One grows as the understanding grows and we move towards acceptance.

I have learned that this is one step that can be worked to perfection. This is true because of the fact that we are asked only to admit to our powerlessness and unmanageability. The step itself does not include the word *acceptance.* The other steps are worded in a manner that dictates that we will never be finished with any of them. We will only be able to make progress with each of them, and they are meant to be a way of life.

Step One is the foundation for a new way of life. It is the one step that we will revisit over and over again as we embark on the journey of the remaining steps. It is the acceptance of our powerlessness and unmanageability that gives us the courage to work the remaining steps to the best of our ability. It is the impetus to persevere when we hit the stumbling blocks along the way.

STEP ONE

SELF-STUDY QUESTIONS

1. What are you powerless over? How has this made your life unmanageable?

2. Make an inventory of events in your life where you were out of control over your addiction or compulsive behavior. Make sure to include your feelings and emotions as well as your behaviors.

3. Make a commitment to ask for help to stay away from one drink, addictive substance, or compulsive behavior for one day at a time. If you have trouble doing this because you don't believe it will work, try doing it "as if you believe" or believe that others believe that this will work for you. Record your experience with this on a daily basis. Journal if you can, but at least jot notes so you can share your experience with others.

4. How have you had to deal with denial in your life? What effects has it had on your quality of life?

5. Describe your acceptance of your powerlessness and unmanageability.

Chapter 2

FINDING HOPE

STEP TWO

WE CAME TO BELIEVE THAT A POWER GREATER THAN OURSELVES COULD RESTORE US TO SANITY.

After admitting to my powerlessness over alcohol, I was blessed to have people share the next two steps with me in a way that I could understand. Admitting powerlessness is a process that can lead to despair if that is the end of the journey. Steps Two and Three are the steps that bring hope to anyone who is committed to recovery from an addiction or compulsive behavior, or who is engaging in spiritual growth. Step Two leads us to a power greater than ourselves, and Step Three initiates a relationship with that power. The first order of business is addressing our need to find power outside of ourselves to accompany us throughout the remaining steps.

> Come, whoever you are!
> Wanderer, Worshipper,
>   Lover of Leaving.
> Come, this is not a caravan of despair.
> It doesn't matter if you've broken your vow a thousand times.
> Still, and yet again, come, come.
> *~Rumi, Sufi poet*

When I first got sober and after I had come to some kind of understanding that I needed help to recover from my disease, the next suggested action was another huge stumbling block. Once I had recognized my powerlessness and unmanageability in my life, despair tried to take over and convince me that I would not be able to stay sober. If you recognize that you are powerless, and there is no way to cope with that reality, then you are without hope. This was one of the many key turning points in my early sobriety and ultimately on my spiritual journey. I was able to continue with my newfound way of life only because there were people who had experience, strength, and hope to share with me and help me understand that there was much more involved than just not picking up a drink. This is why it is critical for all who are daring to embrace these steps in any area of their lives to have some type of support group to help them understand the process.

So the second step is really a step about hope, because there is a way to handle this powerlessness. I needed to find a source where I could find power to help me—something outside of my own self. I would fail if I tried to use my own willpower, self discipline, or any other native strength or ability. I was told that trying to use willpower over something where I had no power was like trying to stop diarrhea once it started! That was quite graphic, but it certainly helped me to understand the concept.

The first words that jumped out at me in this step were "restore us to sanity." In order to be restored to sanity, you had to be "insane." I did not identify this as a term that was applicable to me. Insanity was reserved for those who had mental illnesses and needed to be hospitalized, or "locked up." This certainly was not how I viewed my situation, even though I was having trouble with my drinking. I dared to ask one of the people from the program how this could possibly apply to me. It took great courage on my part even to ask, but I was starting to trust the folks who were there to help me. The woman I asked answered with a question. She said, "Do you think that you have trouble when you drink?" I was honest and admitted that I did have trouble. And then she asked, "And do you still have the desire to drink?" I was somewhat offended by that direct question because I thought the answer was obvious. Why would I be doing all of this searching if I didn't still have the urge to drink? But I tried to stay in the moment and again answered honestly by saying, "Yes, I still have the urge to drink." And then she hit me right between the eyes with the reply, "Well, don't you think it is insane thinking to want to drink if you know that you have trouble when you drink?" She went on to explain that the insanity referenced in Step Two is the thinking that precedes picking up the first drink. If you are successful in taking an honest self-appraisal of your drinking history, and as a result can identify the fact that drinking has caused trouble in your life, then why would any sane and rational human being engage in that activity? Of course, the answer lies in the fact that the powerlessness over the substance or

> The insanity referenced in Step Two is the insanity that precedes picking up the first drink.

activity is what drives us to repeat the insane behavior over and over again. For me to think that I could drink in safety was insane.

After this conversation I was able to come back to the step to read it in its entirety: "Came to believe that a power greater than ourselves could restore us to sanity." Now that I had an understanding of the sanity that I had to address, I had to think about what it was saying to me. The concept seemed simple enough—that there is some power that is greater than I that would restore me to sanity. I wondered how that would happen, but was told that the process of restoring me to sanity was in the third step. For Step Two, I only had to believe that this power existed. What I needed to focus on was coming to believe that it was possible for me to be restored to sane thinking—thinking that did not include picking up a drink.

So now the challenge with this step began. I was told that if I did not believe that there was a power that could do this for me, I had some other options that would help. I was told that if I would continue to come to these people—come and talk, come and listen, come and be present—eventually I would be able to "come to." "Come to" was defined as a phrase that signified waking up, getting some kind of understanding of my life, some semblance of order in my life. I had spent ten years of engaging in behavior that was centered around alcohol and trying to find a "good time." I planned my life around people and events that supported this quest.

So the process of coming to is just that. It is a process. If you continue to come to gatherings of sober people, your brain will wake up. And when your brain wakes up, you come to believe that there is something that is helping others not to drink, and that this is a possibility for you.

I was also told to "believe that we believe." In other words, I couldn't necessarily believe that I could go for a day, a week, or a month without a drink of alcohol. But the people I was talking to said that *they* believed for me. And if I could trust in them and their belief, then one day I would believe for myself.

The next difficulty came with trying to understand *what* I would believe in. The step says, "Came to believe that a power greater than ourselves could restore us to sanity." For me, I grew up in a very religious family—a family that was very focused on the Christian church and a Christian foundation. That foundation was the result of a lot of teaching, a lot of going to church and participating in such things as Bible studies, Christian education, youth groups, worship services, and other functions with my family. During this time I was listening and desperately wanting to believe what I heard. At the same time, I was hearing some things that were not very exciting. I heard about sin, judgment day, and the book of Revelation. I was told that God has a big book where all of my sins are recorded and that one day I would stand face-to-face with God and have to account for my behavior. That was terrifying to me. The religion I was taught resulted in some of the basic fears that I was experiencing in my life when I got sober. It is not important why they were there or whether they were valid. The important thing is that they were very real to me. It is also important to know that all of this information was shared with me because my family believed in its truth. The church's teachings were given to me because my parents believed in them, and they shared them with me because they loved me. It was not intended to harm or scare me.

At the time, I didn't grab hold of the message of grace in my church. I am not saying it wasn't there; I am stating that I didn't integrate that part of the teaching into my thinking.

Therefore, when I starting dealing with these steps and my disease of alcoholism, I had to listen to those who had gone before me in recovery and try not to listen to all of the old childhood tapes that kept playing in my brain. My mentors said repeatedly that there was something greater than me that could help with this destructive alcoholic behavior and that I could get help from this power. But I thought, *why would the God that I heard about as a kid, who wanted people to live according to all of the commandments in the Bible, want to have anything to do with me, one who was living pretty much outside of that box?* They suggested that I use this same process of acceptance from Step One to believe in this power. I didn't have a problem that other people believed in this power—or that this power was able to help them to stay sober. But I did have trouble believing that there was a God who cared about me. I believed I was not worthy of this gift.

I had stepped away from any kind of organized religion, because there was no way I could live up to the expectations or standards I thought were required. The good news that was shared with me from the people in Alcoholics Anonymous was that this step was not talking about the God of my youth; it was talking about the God of my understanding. And so I was encouraged to look around and find some power greater than myself—whether it was through the people who were talking to me or another group of people who were staying sober. I needed to identify something or Someone I could believe in that could help me to maintain my sanity—meaning help me to not pick up one drink for one day. I was not asked to worship that power, or even to talk to that power. I just had to acknowledge that the power existed.

> I needed to identify something I could believe in that could help me to maintain my sanity—meaning help me to not pick up one drink for one day. I was not asked to worship that power, or even to talk to that power. I just had to acknowledge that the power existed.

I did believe that there was something in this universe that was bigger than me. I had become complacent in practicing any formal acknowledgement of that power. But as I stayed away from alcohol and acquired some continuity in this new way of life, I was able to remember what I had always believed. My belief in a power greater than myself had not gone away, it had just been ignored or buried beneath the ramblings of a life lived in pursuit of the false god of my culture—the god of money and power, of satisfaction and happiness found in people, places, and things. This god was not real. And the god that I had created in my mind during my young adulthood was also not real. The God who led me to this new way of life was the God whom I chose to believe existed and chose to believe could restore me to sanity.

STEP TWO

STEP TWO FOR EVERYONE

The insanity that precedes picking up a drink for an alcoholic is the same insanity that exists for anyone dealing with addictive or compulsive behavior. What is referenced in this step is really the kind of insanity that says, "I have power." This way of thinking goes beyond addictive behavior. Many who don't struggle with addiction don't believe they need power outside of themselves unless they have attempted to do the work required in Step One. If they have worked through that step, then they can move on to Step Two.

Think about all that has gone on in your life, whether it is with powerlessness over compulsive spending, gambling, overeating, or any other addictive, compulsive, or destructive behavior. Have you ever thought that you could control these behaviors on your own? Have you ever tried to control your behavior in any way and failed?

We all have insane thinking that speaks lies by encouraging or even justifying our out-of-control behavior. For compulsive eaters, the insanity can take the form of thoughts that lead them to believe that comfort can be found in certain foods. We actually call them "comfort foods." They might be foods that remind us of good memories of our mother's cooking or things that we consumed when we were happy. So when negative emotions are taking over our thinking, we tend to think that food can make us feel better. The insanity leads us to think that food can fight depression, anxiety, or stress. Many of us have conditioned ourselves to the point that we never even stop to think about it—we just react.

The lies can also come in the form of postponement. By that I mean that our thinking can lead us to believe that we can deal with our addictive or compulsive behavior at a later time, and that we can do whatever we want today and start dealing with it tomorrow. Or we say we can't start today because of some compelling reason—it's my birthday, or a holiday, or vacation. There can be a range of excuses for delaying our pursuit of a healthier life style. Unfortunately, our society and culture tend to look negatively at any effort to try to change. So we label healthier eating as "dieting" and stopping drinking as "going on the wagon." And all of these concepts foster the belief that what we are doing is temporary and one day we will fail and return to our old way of life. However we choose to phrase it, the reality is that we have become powerless over a substance or behavior in our life, and until we acknowledge that in the first step and turn to find a power greater than ourselves to help us to return to sanity, we will be without hope for ever finding a permanent and healthy response to our powerlessness.

THE MYSTERY REVEALED IN THE SIMPLICITY OF STEP TWO

> **We find hope when we find power outside of ourselves.**

The mystery that is revealed in the simplicity of Step Two is threefold: Once we *come*—come to being able to ask for help from others—and then when we *come to*—come to where we are able to think clearly about our situation and what is being offered to us as a source for strength—then *we will find hope* in ultimately *coming to believe*—coming to believe that there really is a power that can and will restore us to sanity. A definition of insanity is that we continue to repeat the same behavior over and over again, expecting different results. The sanity is simply the ability to recognize the thinking that precedes our engaging in behavior that is negative and leads to a self-centered, egotistical dependence on something other than a God of grace. This truth applies to all of us—those of us who have addictions and those of us who do not.

STEP TWO

SELF-STUDY QUESTIONS

1. Identify an area in your life where you are powerless. Describe the efforts you have made to try to change your behavior. Describe a time when you thought, "I can change this on my own if I only . . ." and fill in the end of that statement.

2. What thoughts have you experienced with this area of your life that were lies? For example, "I can have one drink and stop," "I am only going to eat what I shouldn't just for today," "I don't care—I will deal with this later (or another day, etc.). How does this translate into insane thinking?

3. Describe how you feel when you are "out of control."

4. Are there any stumbling blocks to your believing that there is a power greater than yourself in this world or universe? If so, what are they?

Chapter 3

MAKING A DECISION

STEP THREE

MADE A DECISION TO TURN OUR WILL AND OUR LIVES OVER TO THE CARE OF GOD AS WE UNDERSTOOD HIM

It was now time for me to move from reflection to action. The first step required me to make an honest appraisal of my life and the role that alcohol had played in it. I had to accept that I was powerless over alcohol, that my life had become unmanageable, and then find a way to believe that something bigger than myself could restore me to a sound mind and accept this newfound knowledge about myself. This reflection helped me to not pick up the first drink. But now, I had to take my first real action step. I had to make a decision and follow through with what I had learned. I came to understand that the remaining effectiveness of all of the steps was dependent upon my success with the first three steps. The final piece of this foundation was to enter into a relationship with a higher power that would provide support for not drinking and for persevering with the remaining steps.

This wasn't easy. I still carried the leftover fear and anxiety from my understanding of the God from my childhood. Turning my will and life over to the care of God was directly related to what is known as an "altar call." In many Christian churches, believers are encouraged to go to the altar of the church, kneel down, and invite Jesus into their hearts. I had done this when I was thirteen years old. I chose to do it

> The grace of God is not dependent upon me; it is totally dependent upon Him—it is a free gift.

because others had done it, and it was expected of me. I certainly never wanted to disappoint my parents in any way, and I also was hopeful that something magical would happen after I took this action. The reality was that there was no great spiritual awakening for me as a result of my decision and action. I do believe that God honors our intentions when they are sincere. And I was sincere in trying to please my parents, but not necessarily in wanting to live in a partnership with the God of their understanding. They had, in real love, tried to help me find God by handing me the versions that worked for them. But I had to find God for myself.

I had learned many of the teachings in the Bible as a child and knew a lot of the Bible stories. What I had failed to do was find a way to establish a personal relationship with God. Perhaps it was because I feared Him. I'm not sure. But I have since learned through my own spiritual journey that God and His grace had been with me every day of my life, whether or not I acknowledged it or felt it. The grace of God is not dependent upon me; it is totally dependent upon Him—it is a free gift.

As I began to learn about the third step, I used my previous success of approaching my understanding of the step in pieces. It worked on the first two steps, and I trusted that it would work once again. The first part of this step is "Made a decision." I learned that I could use my intellect at this point in my sobriety, and that was a great comfort. I didn't have to *feel close* to this higher power, nor did I have to *want* to have a relationship with the God of my understanding. I didn't even have to *believe* that this step would work for me as it had worked for others. But I did have the option to use my brain and evaluate the facts that were placed before me, and then make a decision based on those facts. The facts were these: I was powerless over alcohol, my life was a mess, and I believed that others had found a power greater than themselves that could help them stay sober. Based on these facts, it made sense to me to make a decision to attempt to work Step Three into my life.

So, the making of the decision is the first part of Step Three: I needed to use my brain, use the fact that I did have to have an understanding of what was going on, and realize that I did have a choice. In the past I did not have a choice. Alcohol was making my choices for me. For many people compulsive spending or overeating makes their choices for them. The addiction makes the decision—not the person.

The next part of the step told me what action I would have to take. It states that I am to turn my will and my life over to the care of God. Wow! This is where my mind went back to the altar call. I now know that comparing this step to any religious practice is a false analogy. There is a big difference between this step and an altar call in the Christian church. Step Three has a key phrase that makes the

> Caring meant that I would not be judged for things that I did wrong; it meant nurturing and safety; creating a safe haven. Later I would find out that I would always be accountable for wrongdoing, but never punished for my failings.

difference: "to the care of God." I am to turn my will and my life over to God's care. An altar call is when you kneel down in front of someone and invite Jesus Christ into your heart, which I thought meant that I would completely lose control of my life. I would be asked to become a missionary and go to Africa to "save" those who had not found God. I now know that my interpretation of this was a distorted view of what becoming a Christian meant. But it was important that I understand the difference between this idea and what Step Three said. And when I did, I was able to take a giant step forward in my recovery. By allowing God to "care for" my will and my life, I was surrendering to something of great comfort. The word *care* suggested to me that I would experience a loving presence. I would be the recipient of something wonderful if I took this action. Caring meant that I would not be judged for things that I did wrong; it meant nurturing and safety, a safe haven. Later I would find out that I would always be accountable for wrongdoing, but never punished for my failings.

This new insight provided me with something to hold onto in terms of believing that this process could work for me. I still had to deal with the last part of the step that qualified this God in my mind. It said that I would take this action with the God of *my understanding*. I did not have to use the God of my parents, the Christian God, or the God of anyone else's understanding. It was, and needed to be, the God of *my understanding*. I was fortunate to learn that God has no grandchildren, meaning I cannot have a relationship with my parents' God just because they had a relationship with Him. I had to find my own understanding and build my faith on my own personal experience. I soon found that I did in fact already have an understanding of God and that I was comfortable using that name to describe Him. I had never stopped believing in God—I just struggled with my understanding of His identity. When I started talking to people in Alcoholics Anonymous and listening to their stories, I was able to find a God who was loving, kind, compassionate, and full of mercy.

I saw that in my own life I had experienced His grace—through something that we don't usually associate with grace. I was a daily drinker and had never tried to stay away from alcohol for any reason other than when taking a drug that could have a bad interaction with alcohol. My solution to that problem was not to take the drug! But after having some time not drinking, I realized I had managed to stay sober because of the fear of what would happen if I drank. But that thought helped me see that there was a power greater than me who would use *anything* in my life to help me. The fear was working and was a means of grace that kept me sober until I was of a sound mind and could take the first three steps and practice them to the best of my ability.

I knew that the God who got people sober was a kind and gentle God, and so I was now able to use my intellect to make a decision based on the facts of my own life situation, not on any other person's expectations or desire. After I came to the conclusion that I wanted to move on, I questioned how to put these three steps into my own life—how to translate them into some type of concrete action. I turned once again for advice from the experts who had helped me come this far. This is what I learned.

When I had first approached these folks and asked how to stay sober, they did not overwhelm me with the Twelve Steps and tell me that I had to practice them in order to stay sober and that this was the only solution to the problem. Instead, it was suggested that I should get down on my knees each morning and ask God to help me not pick up one drink, for one day, and that at night I should get back down on my knees and say thank you for the day of sobriety that I had received. This was working the first three steps without understanding them. By getting on my knees and asking for help, I was admitting that I was powerless and that I needed help to not drink. This was enacting Step One and Step Two. When I followed this suggestion, I was acting as if I believed that there was some power greater than me that could keep me sane enough to not drink. By getting down on my knees, I was symbolically "bowing" to this higher being and acknowledging that "it" was bigger and had more power than I did. I learned that I was also making a decision to turn that part of my will and my life over to the care of some power that was bigger than me. I was amazed that this was true, and I started to feel good about myself. I was actually engaged in the power of these steps and I didn't even know it!

As I stayed sober and wanted to learn more, I was also introduced to a prayer taken from the original text of Alcoholics Anonymous. It was suggested that I find someone I trusted who was practicing a spiritual life that I respected to listen to me as I recited the prayer. It made the step more formal for me, and I did it. But the prayer can be read and prayed alone. This prayer is part of a discussion of the third step of the book and can be recited as follows:

> God, I offer myself to Thee—to build with me and to do with me as Thou wilt. Relieve me of the bondage of self, that I may better do Thy will. Take away my difficulties, that victory over them may bear witness to those I would help of Thy Power, Thy Love, and Thy Way of life. May I do Thy will always![2]

I still use this prayer on a regular basis. I have changed the vernacular to be more pleasing to me. But I have not changed the content of the prayer. This is an amazing and powerful prayer. Whenever I am confronted with speaking before others or doing something that requires great courage, I use this prayer. When I am confused about a decision, or fearful of a situation, I use this prayer. When I am concerned that my ego is driving my actions, I use this prayer.

Today I have a new analogy for helping me and others understand the concept of God's care. I use my relationship with my cat, whose name is Allie.

Allie adopted our family when he was somewhere around two years old. He was homeless and found our place to be a safe haven. My role in Allie's life is similar to God's role in my life. I take "care" of Allie by providing food, shelter, and medical coverage for him. He in turn has learned to trust that I will do this for him. He goes out each day and acts very much like a cat. He takes his will with him and lives his life as a cat. I do not interfere with what he does. He stays in our house when there is a storm and jumps when a rumble of thunder goes by. But he knows that he is safe and stays in our care until the storm has passed. Sometimes he gets aggravated with me, and if I approach him in what he perceives to be a threatening move, he swipes at me with his claws. This is not at all pleasant for me, but I do not deny him his care. I still provide his food, shelter, and medical care. He is able to be angry with me, stay away for long periods of time by not coming into the house some nights, and even deny my existence. But he does trust me and always comes home. However, many times he doesn't come when I call him; rather, he comes when he decides he's ready. And so, in this simple analogy I represent the Higher Power, and Allie represents any of us. This seems to help others understand the struggle of surrender. Like Allie, we do not let go of our wills so that they no longer exist, and we do not lose our ability to manage our own lives. We don't always respond to God's call or His care, but He is there waiting for us to make the decision to return to His care. When we do make a decision to let the Higher Power take care of us, He provides for us and guides us so that we are able to follow His lead.

STEP THREE FOR EVERYONE

I came to understand that the God I had started to encounter in this new journey of life was a God of grace—because it was only God's grace that led me to these steps. And if there really is a loving God who cares enough about a group of alcoholics to present to them this incredible program of recovery, then He must be a pretty awesome God. He was not a God who was out to make everything difficult; in fact, He was so full of grace, caring, love, and compassion that He gave these twelve simple steps in language that we could understand. Beyond this amazing truth is the fact that this same grace as experienced through the steps works for all people who seek a new way of life or seek help with any compulsive or addictive behavior or desire a deeper relationship with the God of their understanding.

> This same grace as experienced through the steps works for all people who seek a new way of life.

Jan G.

I have met many people who believe that God is a God who hands out punishments, temptations, and tragedies. There are people who believe that God controls every event in our lives, and ultimately, our death. They make God responsible for every tragedy in this world, such as the death of a young child or the horror of 911. Some question the nature of a God who would not intervene with the Holocaust and stop the brutal killings. Yet they also believe in free will and our ability to make choices in our life. It is amazing how these two thought patterns conflict with each other. If God controls everything that happens to us, then it is indeed a cruel God who allows the tragedies to occur and holds the people responsible for the sin that created the tragedy. The Holocaust was the result of a group of people who chose to follow a leader who was insane. If God should have intervened with that situation, then where do you draw the line of how and when God should intervene to stop intentional actions? Another way of addressing this is to ask how you can hold each party responsible for the tragedy—God and the person or people?

From my own life experience, as well as some theological training, here is how I would address this issue. I believe that God has created each of us with free will to make decisions and engage in our own behaviors, with the ultimate choice to love Him, be in relationship with Him, and to help others know of His love and grace. We are not puppets who are controlled; neither is God absent in any of the decisions or events in our life. People hurt others—either intentionally or inadvertently—and are hurt themselves, because of the free will with which we humans were created. The good news is that God wants all of us to come to Him with all of our hurts and tragedies. He wants everyone in the world to come to Him and His care so that He can love us through the pain we experience and redeem it so it can be used for the good of those involved. This does not mean that tragedy and pain will disappear from our lives or that the memories of past hurts will be removed. Rather, with God's help, we will all have the opportunity to find healing for ourselves and help others to work through similar situations to find the healing love of God.

God also wants to be present in our celebrations. He wants to be included in the happy occasions of marriages, births, graduations, anniversaries, sports victories, and any other event that brings us pleasure. He wants to share in each and every part of our lives, good and bad.

When people attribute certain tragedies to God's will, such as the death of a young child or parent with young children, they are portraying a God who is not loving or compassionate. When given an opportunity, I say to those people, "I wish that you could find the God I have found. Because the God I have found is a God of infinite grace, unconditional love, mercy, and compassion. I believe that my God loves all of us so deeply that He is not about judgment; He is not about punishment. Rather, my God says, 'Come to me because I care, I love, and I want a relationship with you.'" This is the God whom I have continued to encounter for more than thirty years of sobriety. This is the God I have found who loves unconditionally and accepts each one of us just as we are. This is the God I hope others turn their will and their lives over to. Tragedies happen for many reasons, such as sickness, accidents, or war. These are not *sent from* God, but God is *present in* all of these with open arms and an invitation to come into His care.

One of my favorite songs that I have loved since college is a show tune from the Rogers and Hammerstein musical *Carousel*, "You'll Never Walk Alone." The words reflect the spirit of Step Three and were embedded in my spirit even when I was not actively seeking a personal relationship with God. The words still give me comfort and a sense of well-being even as I listen to them, now that I have my own understanding of God and have a very deep relationship with Him.

THE MYSTERY REVEALED IN THE SIMPLICITY OF STEP THREE

> **When we surrender, we win!**

Once the first three steps have been initiated, then everything else is possible in every area of our lives, but especially in our efforts at working the remaining nine steps of this program. When times get tough, or we struggle with one of the steps, there is a simple approach to handling the situation. We once again consciously turn to the principles of Step Three along with the first two steps. Simply stated, we can say out loud or to ourselves, "I can't, He can, I think I will let him." The first three steps are really that uncomplicated. The result of this practice is the mystery of a life that is transformed. We move from the powerlessness that created an unmanageable life to a life filled with hope and the safe haven of a caring God, who will carry us through all of life's difficulties.

The "why" and "how" of this process does not need to be understood; instead, we can grab hold of one of the classic banners that appears in many halls of Alcoholics Anonymous that reads, "But for the grace of God." But for the grace of God, I would not be sober. But for the grace of God, I would not have hope for finding a solution to my powerlessness, unmanageability, and insane thinking. The mystery revealed is that I need to surrender to win! This is totally opposite of what our culture teaches us, yet this is the reality. When I surrender my will and my life to the care of a loving God, then I find the power to live a transformed life that is beyond my understanding.

Jan G.

STEP THREE

SELF-STUDY QUESTIONS

1. Make a list of the facts you have learned about your own powerlessness, unmanageability, and insane thinking.

2. What does the word *care* mean to you? Describe how it feels to be cared for.

3. Describe the God of your understanding. Describe how this understanding came into your life.

4. Where have you experienced the grace of God in your life or in the life of someone you know?

5. Do you have any objections to turning your will and your life over to the care of God? If so, what are they? If not, why not?

Chapter 4

TAKING INVENTORY

STEP FOUR

MADE A SEARCHING AND FEARLESS MORAL INVENTORY OF OURSELVES

After I became comfortable with my newfound relationship with God, I was very eager to "get on" with the program of recovery as suggested in the Twelve Steps. I continued to listen to those who had been able to stay sober and live by the principles of the steps. I wanted the peace of mind and serenity that they radiated. I wanted to grow into the kind of person they encouraged me to believe was my true self. Although I was told that this type of growth and change would take time, I was as obsessed with this new concept of life as I had been with my addiction to alcohol. I wanted it all, and I did not want to have to wait. The hope that I acquired in the first three steps welled up inside of me, and I wanted to do everything that I could to reap the benefits of long-term sobriety in a short amount of time. Do I need to state that this was *not* going to happen as I planned?

I was not so very different from others who had gone before me. I came to understand that the very nature of an alcoholic includes the basic flaw of impulsiveness and lack of patience. I now think that these characteristics are really part of the human condition, but just exaggerated in the alcoholic. Nevertheless, I immediately engaged

> The problem with people who have no vices is that generally you can be pretty sure they're going to have some pretty annoying virtues.
> *~Elizabeth Taylor*

in trying to accomplish ten years of sobriety in less than one! I listened to my mentors with great earnestness so that I could learn from them and not repeat their mistakes. I was determined to work the remaining steps as quickly as possible and without flaw.

As I listened to stories of how people worked the fourth step, I heard many people talk about how they had delayed this step because of fear. The step suggests that we make a "searching and fearless moral inventory of ourselves." I did not understand what would define a moral inventory and was not sure why people were so afraid of doing this work. But as I listened, it became clear that for some people it is very difficult to look at their past behaviors and events that might have caused harm or injury to others. I began to understand that the word *moral* was used to talk about right and wrong behavior.

Twelve Steps and Twelve Traditions (which I'll refer to as the *Twelve and Twelve* in the rest of the book) introduces the discussion of this step by stating that "nearly every serious emotional problem can be seen as a case of misdirected instinct."[3] When Bill Wilson and Dr. Bob Smith first found each other and shared their stories, they came to understand that they would need to clear the "wreckage of their past" in order to stay sober. It doesn't take much understanding and very little wisdom to know that we all carry "baggage"—or memories—of things we have done that we regret. This baggage can be extremely dangerous for an alcoholic. Guilt and shame can be strong motivators to drink, in order to anesthetize the pain from these feelings. The two pioneers in the AA program realized this and found that by sharing these memories they received a freedom and somehow reduced the burden of guilt and shame. Over the years, their followers also found this to be true, and when the steps were finally put onto paper, they included this key foundation for sobriety—a searching and fearless moral inventory.

Many alcoholics think they can drink to forget their past. The reality is that often the drinking to forget leads to other tragedies that increase the list of wrongdoings. As the program matured with time, the original members discovered that putting these items on a written list helped them perform this very necessary personal "house cleaning." When I learned about the intent of the step, I thought I knew how to do it from listening to others discuss their experience. But when I put my pen to paper and tried to make my own personal list, I discovered that I was not ready to approach this kind of thorough searching of my past in my first year of recovery. There are many treatment programs today that require the participants to make this list as part of their therapy. I was not afforded the opportunity of a treatment program. However, I do know with great certainty, that the concept that I came to believe concerning God's response to our efforts is a universal truth—God honors our best intentions.

There is no one way to get sober or to stay sober. Every path of recovery is as unique as the individual pursuing it. There are some fundamental principles that cannot be violated—such as the principle of not picking up a drink. There are other fundamental principles that affect the quality of one's sobriety, such as a persistent and sincere effort to learn, understand, and live the steps as they are suggested. This might or might not determine if a person drinks again, but it will definitely impact the way they live their life. Many people who choose not to drink and also choose to ignore the suggestions of the Twelve Steps often live without serenity. I have learned to cherish the wisdom of those who have gone before me. I often question this wisdom, or resist it, or wish it were not true, but I know from my own experience and the experience of others that the wisdom that exists in the collective body of followers of the Twelve Steps has survived the test of time. It is solid, and I am most successful when I choose to follow the suggestions offered from this wisdom.

> You gain strength, experience, and confidence by every experience where you stop to look fear in the face. You must do the thing you cannot do.
> ~Eleanor Roosevelt

This leads me to the conclusion that if one is to have a successful recovery, then he or she should make a list of past wrongdoings. It must be completed when the time is right for each of us. For me, I sat with a new pen, a new notebook, and the *Alcoholics Anonymous* text that gave a suggested format for the list. I tried with as much courage as I could muster, but had minimal results. This is not because I had nothing to go onto the list. Rather, it was because I was lacking trust in the God whom I had found in sobriety. I ultimately discovered that I needed to know that I was loved and accepted by God just as I was. I could not do anything to earn the grace that got me sober, or to become worthy of the grace that was keeping me sober. I needed to learn that if I took a searching and fearless moral inventory of my past behavior, I would not be rejected by this loving God. But at this point, I was feeling the fear that I had heard others allude to as they talked of their own experience.

This fearful part of my recovery was during the time when I was still trying to understand and learn to work the first three steps. Without that foundation, I was floundering with no ability to write a fourth step inventory.

It was after a full year in recovery when I finally was able to put pen to paper and make progress with this step. It took me that long to learn that I was not going to be judged or rejected. I saw others who got sober before me and those who got sober after me, and all of their stories were stories of grace. They were alcoholics who were given the gift of sobriety without earning it. For whatever reason, God has poured out His grace on all people. It is when we become open to this grace that miracles can happen. Repeatedly I heard about God's grace, and through the stories of others I was able to believe that mine was no different. People shared their own wrongdoings and talked of how they stayed sober by following the Twelve Steps. The grace that got them sober kept them sober and provided a path of healing for not only the disease of addiction to alcohol but also for many of the hurts from their past. Once again, it was as a result of these small groups of courageous souls who shared their experience, strength, and hope that I was able to gain enough trust for my own courageous efforts.

I started working with a woman who had the type of recovery that I aspired to attain. She had been diligent in working the steps of the program and shared her wisdom with me on an individual basis. It was important that I work with someone in order to assure that I remain objective and not become overwhelmed with the emotions that would result from this honest self appraisal. I also needed guidance in making sure that I was being completely honest and not blaming others for my behavior. Regardless of the motivation for my actions, I was responsible for what I had done and the results of these actions. My disease had caused me to do things that I would not have chosen to do had I been sober, and have not chosen to do since I began my recovery. I had to learn that, even though I did these things as a person suffering from a debilitating disease, I was still responsible for the outcome of these actions. I had to sort through all of this information when I proceeded to Step Five.

Here is how the main text of *Alcoholics Anonymous* expresses it:

> Putting out of our minds the wrongs others had done, we resolutely looked for our own mistakes. Where had we been selfish, dishonest, self-seeking and frightened? Though a situation had not been entirely our fault, we tried to disregard the other person involved entirely. Where were we to blame? The inventory was ours, not the other man's. When we saw our faults we listed them. We placed them before us in black and white. We admitted our wrongs honestly and were willing to set these matters straight.[4]

This paragraph contained much helpful information for guiding me in this effort. It was especially important to understand that I had to keep the focus on myself and not engage in a "blame game" that would absolve me of my responsibility for my wrongs.

Another important suggestion that helped me focus better on Step Four was that I should try to separate Step Four from Step Five, in which I would be required to share this information with another person. The shame and guilt associated with our wrongdoings can play havoc with us when we think about sharing this list with another person. Step Five is simply not part of Step Four. It is imperative not to think about sharing this information that we are getting ready to put onto paper.

This does not mean that we can't share with someone as we proceed with our list. We are encouraged to ask questions about the process or discuss anything we feel compelled to share that is causing us difficulty. For instance, we might be questioning the inclusion of something on our list, or need to talk about something that begins really to bother us. This is especially important if shame or guilt is building momentum in our lives and we are in danger of drinking because of it.

You can never put too much information on this kind of list, so if you have a question about including a certain event, then put it on the list. Our primary concern should be that we not rationalize and create a reason to keep something off the list because of our underlying fear, shame, or guilt. The disease of alcoholism can scramble our thinking and ability to make good decisions. Therefore, if we are trusting in God to guide us through this process, then we must trust that any memory we have as we are writing should be included.

I was able to begin making my list by following a suggestion to read the text of *Twelve and Twelve* for Step Four. In this text, questions are posed for the reader to ponder in regard to past behavior. We are advised to look at the memories from our past that haunt us the most. We don't have to be concerned with every wrong we have ever done; the process of Step Four will be a lifelong experience. Because of my tendency towards perfectionism, this was a challenge. Once I made a commitment to pursue this step, I wanted to do it as thoroughly as possible. It was good to have a guide who could remind me to stay focused on the task at hand and to trust that God would help me with the process.

The key to Step Four was the foundation that had been laid in Step Three. I had to continue to make a decision to turn my will and life over to the care of God—and to trust that the same care that kept me sober would care for me while doing this inventory. As I sat to write my inventory I would always begin by praying the third-step prayer. It became especially important to me when I asked God to "remove the bondage of self." It was this bondage that I was trying to identify and offer to Him to help me to heal.

The questions from *Twelve Steps and Twelve Traditions* asked me to examine my behavior in relationships, identifying where I had been selfish and how I had been hurtful to others. I tried to examine my behavior concerning financial and emotional security and identify times when fear, greed, possessiveness, or pride had influenced my actions. I learned from the text that "the most common symptoms of emotional insecurity are worry, anger, self-pity, and depression."[5] This was amazing information to me and helped me to look at past situations where these symptoms were dominant in my life. I came to understand that insecurity is a basic human response when we are threatened by outside circumstances, such as loss of job or a broken relationship. These were experiences that had left me feeling lonely and depressed, and I needed to look at them and try to identify where I might have been at fault. I needed to find a way to look past the hurt and pain that caused me to blame others and find where I might have contributed to the situation.

My experience has taught me one important fact about the Fourth Step. I have learned that I will remain a victim of myself and in bondage to myself and my past if I do not engage in this type of honest self-appraisal. I might get temporary relief by blaming another person or situation for my discomfort or pain, but I will only be free of these negative feelings when I examine my own responses. What precipitated my own actions? What behavior was I responsible for, and what could I change in the future? I have now come to treasure this process as a way to peace of mind and serenity. Denial of my past will only allow it to dictate my responses to the present. I also learned that if I allow this denial to continue, then I will become victim to the results of these buried memories when I continue to choose behaviors that will hurt me or others.

This information gathering was not a magical healing potion. The healing would come as I continued to pursue the remaining steps. But I could not address a problem that needed to be fixed until I first identified it. I was assured throughout the process from my mentor and guide that I was not a bad person because of what I had done or because of what I had experienced. In order to help balance this type of over-reaction to taking an inventory, my mentor also encouraged me to complete the inventory by listing those things about myself that are assets. I did not have a lifetime of wrongdoing—there were many things I did that were good.

Twelve and Twelve concludes the discussion of this step with the following statement:

> As we persist, a brand new kind of confidence is born, and the sense of relief at finally facing ourselves is indescribable. These are the first fruits of Step Four.[6]

It amazed me that this became my reality. I did in fact experience a new confidence that remains with me today. I now know that there is nothing to fear from my past, only knowledge to gain that will guarantee me a better future. I no longer fear my own mind, memories, or personality. I believe that I have learned incredible and valuable information about myself that enables me to live a life of freedom from bondage to my past.

STEP FOUR FOR EVERYONE

There is no doubt that the task of writing a searching and fearless moral inventory is difficult. I have observed that the only people who have successfully completed this life-changing work are people in recovery, people in therapy who are trying to grow emotionally and psychologically, and those individuals who are committed to a life of sincere spiritual discipline.

It is easy to assume that this type of inventory is only applicable to those who suffer from an addiction to alcohol or drugs since these diseases are often accompanied by stories of people doing atrocious things as a result of being drunk or getting high. But any human behavior other than alcoholism that becomes addictive or results in an unmanageable life style will also have baggage that can cause one to wallow in despair, guilt, or self-pity. Yet adding people with these problems to the mix does not complete the list of those who need to apply the principle of self assessment to their lives. Self-assessment has been accepted in all great religions as a practice that is critical to achieving any kind of spiritual growth and meaningful relationship with God. The truth is that all human beings benefit from this process of self-searching.

> Your vision will become clear only when you look into your heart. Who looks outside, dreams. Who looks inside, awakens.
> ~ Carl Jung

If you seek to change from who you are to what you were created to be, then you need a clear idea of your starting place. When taking a trip, you can only get reliable directions if you know where you are starting from. To grow in the process of these Twelve Steps, you need to accept the fact that you are who you are at the time of taking the inventory without any sense of blame for how or why you are this person. You cannot change what you cannot accept.

Another pitfall to an honest moral inventory can be the delusion that "we aren't that bad." The reality is that no one is bad, including those who suffer from addiction. We were created with the ability to make bad decisions and bad choices, and to do bad things, but no one is created as a "bad person." We are created by our Higher Power and are all human. The human condition dictates that we will not be perfect, and therefore each of us has caused harm to ourselves or others. In order to live a life of joy and peace, it is imperative that we are free from any guilt or shame that we might carry with us. In order to experience the gift of God's grace working in our lives to the greatest extent possible, we must rid ourselves of this baggage that we all carry. It is a psychological truth that we will continue to repeat patterns of behavior that are driven by underlying difficulties that are not part of our consciousness.

When we have problems that we have not dealt with appropriately, the effects of those problems can come out "sideways." What I mean by this is that many times our decisions in life, or our involuntary actions or reactions are directly related to events or memories from our past. This sideways behavior can result in patterns of repeated actions that baffle us, and leave us questioning why we continue to repeat things that cause us difficulty. Many times the causes of this sideways behavior are not available to our consciousness and are only discovered through a searching and fearless moral inventory accompanied with the remaining twelve step principles. This is a universal truth.

Therefore, the principle of taking a moral inventory is not solely related to those events, actions, or memories only associated with drinking or drug behavior. Addicts, as well as all people attempting this inventory, must examine their entire life story. Many have perhaps had a lifetime of confession as part of their religious upbringing and believe that this step would not be necessary for them. This is not true. The value of this step is that, once taken with painstaking perseverance and discipline, it will become a list of our entire life experience that will often lead to our ability to assess patterns of behavior and discover the source of those patterns. Prior attempts to assess our isolated individual actions or reactions to life might not reveal the truth that can only be discovered when seeing a larger view of our past.

After I completed the list and moved on with the other steps, I continued with the concept of self-examination while working with a therapist. After I was able to move past the items that caused me the greatest difficulty and were most available in my conscious mind, I was able to look further. As time passed, my strength and confidence increased, and I was able to look further into my past and ultimately receive great healing. I came to understand that true freedom to live life in the fullest can only happen when this type of self-assessment is repeated on a regular basis. I gain new insights and gather new information about myself as my trust and dependence upon my Higher Power grows in strength. I believe that God allows me to see only that which I can comprehend and handle emotionally at any given time. Today I believe that there are no longer any unknown ghosts from the past that can haunt me or influence my behavior.

Those who are not part of a program of recovery will benefit from using the same inventory process that is used in the various programs of recovery. A partial and general list of questions that can be used for starting the process is included in the study guide at the end of this chapter. There are many online resources for providing a format and guidance for doing this inventory, as well. The following websites provide an actual guide and worksheets.

http://www.step12.com/step-4.html
http://theserooms.blogspot.com/2004/11/online-fourth-step-resources.html

The following quote from the first web-site summarizes the power and purpose of the suggested moral inventory.

> Step Four is a fact-finding and fact-facing process. We are searching for "causes and conditions."

We want to uncover the truth about ourselves. We want to discover the attitudes, thoughts, beliefs, fears, actions, behaviors, and behavior patterns that have been blocking us and creating problems that can lead to our failure. We want to learn the exact nature of our "character defects" and what causes us to do the unacceptable things we do. Then when these defects are removed, we will develop new attitudes, thoughts, and beliefs, and our actions and behaviors will change for our highest good and the highest good of those with whom we come in contact.

This prepares us to live lives of purpose, where we can be in maximum fit condition to be of service to others. And by taking inventory and learning the exact nature of our wrongs, we will be able to recognize when we might be slipping into our old way of life and headed for new problems, and possibly relapse.

If you doubt that you have any problems, just think back to the last time you felt restless, irritable, and discontented. Remember when you got angry—with your self or with another person. Remember the last time you were disturbed. Remember the last time you had a problem or troubles. The last time you felt uncomfortable and not at ease in a situation. What was it? Who was it with? What happened?

THE MYSTERY REVEALED IN THE SIMPLICITY OF STEP FOUR

> **The freedom in life does not come from burying our past, our fears, or anxieties; rather the freedom comes when we embrace them and deal with them directly.**

We are victims of our own past until we find our own truth, acknowledge it, confront it, and embrace it. The simple act of writing a list helps us to think clearly and do an honest appraisal. The true simplicity in the mystery of Step Four is the same simple concept that Franklin D. Roosevelt stated at the beginning of World War II: "We have nothing to fear but fear itself." Freedom in life does not come from burying our past, our fears, or anxieties; rather, freedom comes when we embrace them and deal with them directly. We will not be free from our bondage until we can identify our bondage. When we do, and when we confront it, we are able to let go.

STEP FOUR

SELF-STUDY QUESTIONS

1. Research the internet and find a fourth step guide that you can use to complete your inventory.

2. Identify a person who has completed a fourth step and contact that person. Ask if you can meet to discuss this process. If you like what the person shares, ask if you can use him or her as a resource while you complete this inventory.

3. As a primer to the inventory, write your answers to the following questions, which are based on questions presented in the *Twelve Steps and Twelve Traditions*.

    a. Relationships

        i. List any personal relationship that brought continuous or recurring trouble. How have I been at fault? If I was not at fault, why did I accept the behavior that harmed me?

ii. When, how, and in just what instances did my own selfish desires damage my relationship with other people, including family and friends? What people were hurt, and how badly?

iii. Did I ever cause harm to my marriage or injure my children? When? How?

iv. Did I ever jeopardize my standing in my community? When? How?

v. How did I react to the above situations that I just described? Did I feel guilt? Or did I insist that I only reacted to others and that I was not responsible?

vi. How have I reacted to frustration in sexual matters? When denied, did I become vengeful or depressed? Did I "take it out" on other people? When I was rejected, did I use this as a reason for promiscuity?

b. Financial and emotional security: survey your business or employment record and answer the following

i. When have I suffered from financial instability? How did I contribute to this situation?

ii. Have I ever cheated, lied, or evaded responsibility? How? When?

iii. Did I ever overvalue myself and "play the big shot"? How? When?

iv. Did I ever double-cross or undercut my associates? How? When?

v. Was I extravagant in my spending? How? When?

vi. Did I ever recklessly borrow money? How? When?

Chapter 5

FINDING FREEDOM

STEP FIVE

ADMITTED TO GOD, TO OURSELVES, AND TO ANOTHER HUMAN BEING THE EXACT NATURE OF OUR WRONGS

Step Five presented a whole new challenge in the twelve-step journey. This step requires that the information gathered in Step Four be shared with God *and* another human being. I had no problem thinking about sharing this inventory with God since I had asked for Him to help me identify what I needed to put on my list. My concept of God included an omniscient quality, or One possessing knowledge of everything in this world, including all of my sins, or character defects, as labeled by the Alcoholics Anonymous literature. So sharing with God did not seem as if it would be difficult, although I was not sure how to pursue that disclosure. In fact, I questioned why I would even need to admit the things on my list to Him since He already knew them anyway.

It also seemed odd to me that I would have to exercise some type of admission of this information to myself. Wasn't I the one who wrote the content of the inventory? This made no sense to me that I should have to "admit" something to myself that I obviously already knew.

But the greatest hurdle to overcome was the fear that accompanied the idea of sharing all of this information with another person. One of the greatest fears in my life was the fear of being rejected. I was convinced, because I did not like who I was, that anyone who really got to know me would surely reject me too. I could think of nothing greater to fear. I certainly had secrets that I shared with no one for that very reason. And now I was being asked and encouraged to take this incredible risk in sobriety.

It is here that I had to learn a fundamental principle that would be applied to my first attempt at this step and all of my efforts with the remaining steps. The principle that emerged was that I would need to rely on my foundation of the first step to help me find courage to take the remaining actions in this journey when those actions appeared too difficult, or when I simply did not want to do them. I was advised to remember the contents of the fourth step inventory and think about the consequences of drinking again. I listened to the stories of people who did not do fourth and fifth steps and ultimately relapsed into their disease. I listened to the stories of people who had the courage to do this work and heard them describe the freedom they had found as a result of this fifth-step process. All of the steps provide a kind of freedom, but I was hearing that it was during this particular step that many found the greatest freedom and release from their bondage to self. This is the step that helps provide the pathway to the third-step prayer when we ask for release from our bondage to self. The principle of remembering my powerlessness and unmanageability, as identified during my first step, provided motivation to pursue the next step that was in front of me. The willingness to take a fifth step was derived from the knowledge I had found while doing the inventory in my first step, and my desire to stay sober as a result of my acceptance of my disease. I did not want to relapse and I had not heard of one person relapsing who had tried to do a searching and fearless moral inventory and then share it with God and another person.

And so I used what I learned in the Step Three, the tool of making a decision based on fact and not on feeling. I remembered that I had turned my will and my life over to the care of God and that I was loved unconditionally by Him. With that comforting thought, I looked for a way to share the information with Him, with myself, and with another human being. By the time that I was ready to do the Step Five, I was involved in the Episcopal church. I was preparing to go away for a spiritual retreat and decided that I would do a confession with a priest. This was a way that was meaningful to me, in terms of sharing the fourth-step inventory in a more formal way with God than just acknowledging that surely He must know this information since He was omniscient. When I made my decision to move forward with this step, I wanted to make sure that it was thorough.

I do believe that it is important to share the information with God in some

> You can search throughout the entire universe for someone who is more deserving of love than you are yourself, and that person is not to be found anywhere. You yourself, as much as anybody in the entire universe, deserve your love and affection.
> ~Buddha

type of structured manner. The benefit of doing this for me was to understand that God not only knows me and all of my faults, but that He loves me and accepts me unconditionally. This concept emerged during the first three steps, but it became solidified in this sharing of my fourth-step inventory with Him through a confession. It was the first time I offered all of myself with an understanding of who I am to the God of my understanding. This was obviously not a total picture by any stretch of the imagination. But it was, once again, something that I had worked on and truly did to the best of my ability. I did not take any short cuts or leave out anything that I chose to censor. If a wrongdoing came to my consciousness, I put it down on my inventory. And so I offered this information to God as well as to myself during that confession.

It was obvious that by sharing my inventory with the priest that I had also satisfied the last part of the step where it states that we admitted to another human being the exact nature of our wrongs. However, I decided that this was not sufficient for me. I was aware that a priest functions during a confession as a professional. Since one of my shortcomings was the fear of rejection, it was important to share with someone who I knew would not be functioning in a professional role. I needed to be with someone who could indeed reject me if he or she chose to do so after hearing my inventory, someone who would continue to be in my life. Many people use their sponsors in the program, but I chose to use a friend outside of the program—someone who was also attending the retreat. So I met with her following my confession and read my inventory to her. To my great relief, she didn't reject me! I was not rejected by God, the priest, or my friend. What an amazing day! I was exhausted from the emotional strain of the preparations and expectations that I had encountered leading up to this day. But I was also filled with an incredible amount of self-satisfaction at having completed a major step towards growing in sobriety. Calm had settled in that I had never known before. Hindsight tells me that I was finally coming to another level of acceptance of myself, an acceptance that was accompanied by a sense of freedom. This was another level of being freed from the bondage of my past and of my disease.

One of the benefits of sharing with other human beings is the feedback we receive. I did a "searching and fearless moral inventory," but I did it from my perspective. It was wonderful to have two other people react to my perceptions. Many of the comments they made helped me see the true extent of wrongs that I had committed. They also helped me understand that some ownership needed to be shifted from me to the other person—that I had been reacting to a circumstance or situation and had not been guilty for what I had done. However, I was still responsible for my actions. This was important to know and understand. My disease dictated many of my wrongdoings as a result of its interaction with my decision-making capabilities. Yet I had still done these things and needed to make restitution at a later time. Without sharing with another person or persons, I never would have been able to understand this concept or do an honest appraisal of my inventory.

I had heard in the beginning of my sobriety that "we are as sick as our secrets." This is so true. I had been soul sick and in bondage to the fear of who I was and what I had done in my life. The process of sharing with God and with others has proven to be one of the greatest benefits of my sobriety. I know today that I am not alone unless I choose to be. I do not have to live in the self-constructed prison that I occupied for years. As I stayed sober, I was able to continue to go deeper and deeper into the parts of my past that caused me difficulty. Some compare Step Five and the twelve-step journey to the process of peeling an onion layer by layer. We can only confront the "layer" of information that is presented to us in our consciousness at any given moment. We really cannot address all of our issues, concerns, or defects of character without removing the big ones first. After this is accomplished and as we continue to live our lives of new-found freedom, other issues will surface. The key for me is to have a group of trusted friends and spiritual guides with whom I can share my fears, anxieties, and confusion on a routine basis, or as they surface in my life.

I have only made one formal fourth-step inventory, and one formal fifth-step to share the inventory. Many people in recovery choose to do more than one fourth-step, and some do one on an annual basis. But I have incorporated the principles of rigorous honesty in identifying my own character flaws, sins, and defects into my regular routine of life. I have always attempted to share this information with others so that the power of my own fear of rejection and my own secrets will not have an opportunity to control me.

I was also able to see that these principles had been part of my journey prior to the actual fourth and fifth steps. I had already started to share some of my secrets with my sponsor and mentor early in sobriety. There was one haunting facet of myself that I needed to share with her. I believed that this secret was so terrible that sooner or later someone would tell me that I could no longer meet with these people, and that they would no longer be able to help me with my journey of recovery. I decided that if I was going to be rejected, I needed it to happen quickly so that I could stop obsessing and get back to drinking. And so I met with her one day and sat in her car overlooking the ocean. It was a very serene setting, and I took forever to get to what I had to say. But when I finally shared with her this devastating issue in my life, she looked at me and simply said, "Is that all? This is not an issue!" I was incredibly relieved and felt a joy that I could not articulate. As a matter of fact, since I was so newly sober, I was not even able to name the emotion of joy. I just know today with a very grateful heart that this is what happened on that wonderful day: I was filled with an amazing sense of joy and relief. And this experience was truly a reflection of the principles and the intents of the fourth and fifth steps. If I had not chosen to share that information, I am sure that at some point my disease would have ambushed me into thinking that I was unique because of this secret, and therefore, I could not stay sober. So why not go ahead and drink and forget this idea of sobriety?

The fifth step was a true beginning to the end of the isolation I had lived in my entire life. I began to feel as if I had hope that I was not a bad or defective person. I started to believe that I would be able to stay sober and live my life in concert with the principles of the Twelve Steps. It was at a minimum a turning point and a major milestone in my recovery.

STEP FIVE FOR EVERYONE

The beauty of the steps is that they are adaptable for anyone who is willing to pursue them with honesty and perseverance. Over time, I have come to understand that all humans are imperfect, have character defects, make mistakes, and do things they regret. Also, they have an imperfect image of themselves. I learned that I am not as good as others think I am, but I am also not as bad as I think I am. So the question becomes, how do we find out the truth about our wrongdoings? How are we to discern what is a valid opinion about our character and our behavior? What actions are we responsible for, and which ones require restitution for harm that we might have caused others?

Therefore, Step Five is not only applicable to those who have committed some huge wrongdoing; sharing a moral inventory is one of the many spiritual practices that benefits all of us. Unfortunately, it is also an action that is usually taken when a person is in some type of emotional or spiritual pain and seeking relief from that pain. I have yet to find a motivator that can inspire all people to engage in this practice on a regular basis other than returning to something that is equivalent to the Step One inventory that identifies our powerlessness. The Roman Catholic Church and other faiths have included this concept in their practice of confession for centuries. Although I am not a member of this faith tradition, I have observed over the years that there seem to be relatively few practicing Roman Catholics who use this sacrament on a regular basis with the approach of one who is seeking a deeper knowledge of themselves or freedom from their "bondage to self." Rather, for many, confession has become a routine that has lost its meaning and is exercised more out of fear of some type of dire circumstance if they do not do it regularly, rather than because of a desire to grow in their faith or in their spiritual life. Regardless of the motivation, there is no denying that this type of discipline is difficult and can create some emotional and spiritual pain as we risk sharing our inner lives.

There is a phrase I learned along the way that I love, and I think it addresses the reason for one to pursue Steps Four and Five: "The truth will set you free, but first it will make you miserable." When I researched the origin of this phrase, I found that it was a quote from James Garfield, the twentieth President of the United States. There is no source for the quote, so I do not know in what context he was stating this wisdom. I do know that it totally embodies the spirit and intent of the Fifth Step.

It is an absolute truth that we are not capable of making an honest assessment of our own moral character and behavior without the help of another person. I believe that this is true, because it is impossible to be totally objective about our own issues or defects. I believe that those who do not have the benefit of a program should seek counsel from a spiritual director or therapist if they do not have a faith community. Step Five and the concept of self examination is embraced not only in the principles and tenets of the Christian religion, but in psychotherapy and all spiritual disciplines. People who do not engage in this practice are missing an amazing opportunity to know themselves in a new and profound way.

Step Five is also directly connected to humility, which is not in any way related to humiliation. Humiliation is a negative concept that emerges out of shame during some event in our lives. Humility, though, is seeking to become who and what God created us to be. We are self-deceived when we view ourselves as one who does no wrong, or one who is highly successful and therefore should be admired by all. However, the flip side of the coin is also true. We are self-deceived when we think of ourselves as faulty in some way, or less important or significant than other human beings. As it states in the Declaration of Independence, "all men are created equal." This is referencing our "unalienable rights," but I believe that it goes much further than this concept. We are created equal in terms of the quality of our being. There is no one who is better or worse than another. We definitely have different talents and capabilities, but in terms of character, we are all given the same gifts. How we choose to use these gifts can influence how we are viewed by others. Certainly Hitler was a very gifted leader and motivator of people. The problem was not with his giftedness, the problem was how he used this gift and his vision for what he wanted to achieve.

We must all search for a way to communicate with the God of our understanding that we discovered in the first three steps and to identify a process for sharing with God and another person the exact nature of our wrongs. My own experience is that it is most effective for me to use some type of meaningful ritual. Others, both inside as well as outside of a recovery program, have confirmed this approach works for them, as well. If confession is part of your faith tradition, then I recommend that you incorporate this step into that practice. If you don't have a predefined practice that would work, then I recommend that you pay attention to how you perform your third step on a daily basis and observe how that communication occurs. You might also talk with others who are not of the Christian faith to find out how they proceed with this part of Step Five. And finally, you could formally invite the God of your understanding to participate in the sharing of your inventory with whomever you choose to listen to you.

The person you choose to hear your inventory should be someone familiar with the practice of this type of sensitive self disclosure and one who is able to provide feedback from an impartial perspective. The key to Step Five is for you to be able to walk away from such a session with a clear understanding of your responsibility for any wrongs that you have done. It is not intended to make you feel guilty, ashamed, or bad. Therefore, you should select this person with great care.

Step Five is a critical step to attaining the ultimate benefits of the Twelve Steps. If you can muster the courage to pursue this step with integrity and commitment, then the foundation for your success will be in place. It is at this point that the knowledge of unconditional love begins to take root, and true freedom to be the person God created you to be begins to grow. It offers some of the greatest benefits of this spiritual journey.

THE MYSTERY REVEALED IN THE SIMPLICITY OF STEP FIVE

> **We will only be free when we are no longer in bondage to the fear of our secrets being known.**

The keys to completing a fifth step successfully are honesty and perspective. Honesty is required of the one taking the step, and perspective is contributed by another human being in the process. The mystery in this step for those of us who fear having others find out about our secrets is that we will no longer be free to continue our relationships with them until we reveal the truth. The mystery is the simple fact that we will only be free when we are no longer in bondage to the fear of our secrets being known. The fear is overcome when we share our wrongdoings and receive another's perspective concerning these actions. It is the input from another that will give us the desired freedom from our fears and our bondage to our self. It is the sharing of the secrets that we fear; yet it is ultimately the sharing of these secrets that grants us freedom.

STEP FIVE

SELF-STUDY QUESTIONS

1. What objections do you have, if any, to completing a Fifth Step? If you have no objections, then describe why you are comfortable with beginning this step.

2. What are your expectations of completing this step?.

3. What ritual will you use to share your fourth-step inventory with the God of your understanding? How will you proceed with this ritual?

4. Identify the qualities that you will be seeking in someone you will choose to share your fourth step. Make a list of people who you will consider.

Chapter 6

RESPONDING WITH A NEW ATTITUDE

STEP SIX

WERE ENTIRELY READY TO HAVE GOD REMOVE ALL THESE DEFECTS OF CHARACTER

The foundation for a new life is based on the first five steps. I discovered that after I was able to muster the courage to follow these suggested steps to the best of my ability, with honesty, courage, and integrity, then it was time to move to another level of recovery. The first three steps provided me with a relationship with a higher power that enabled me to gain an understanding of unconditional love and acceptance, so I could move forward with the strength and power to begin to have a right relationship with myself. This new relationship was based on the truth of who I am, what I had done and left undone, and insight from at least one other human being to validate my perceptions. The Step Four inventory addressed actions in my life that I was responsible for doing. During the process of sharing with God and another human being, I concluded this part of my journey with a basic understanding of the underlying circumstances that motivated these actions. For example, I found that I had been overly dependent upon others for letting me know that I was okay, because I did not have the self-acceptance I needed to affirm myself. I learned that I did not have to fear rejection by other people because I was loved unconditionally by God.

Step Six offered another level of self examination as I prepared for additional changes I would need to make in my life. When I first started to attend meetings that discussed the Twelve Steps, this step appeared to be lacking substance. I was not able to find any action that would be required. It almost seemed to be a placeholder in the recovery process, and I wondered why it was there. I thought that maybe someone decided that the number of steps should be twelve for some reason, and they added this one to fill a gap when they were short on steps! Little did I know or understand the true intent of the step or the process it involved.

It took me several years of listening and reading about the Twelve Steps before I was able to grasp the concept of Step Six. I actually had to complete the first five steps before it truly had any meaning for me. But ultimately, after sharing my inventory with others and searching for the causes of my behavior, I came to understand why this step was important. The fourth and fifth steps helped me to see and comprehend the parts of my life that I had summarized on paper. By regularly listening to others share about their experiences in recovery, thinking about how their experiences might apply to me, examining myself, and then asking for feedback regarding my own behavior, I gained a better understanding of patterns of behavior that had caused me difficulty. After discovering these patterns and learning how to identify them to myself and others, I had to make a decision about what to do with them. Did I want to continue to repeat these patterns, or did I want to be free from them? Once I had the knowledge of my defects, I was on dangerous ground and setting myself up for a relapse if I chose to ignore them. I was told that I needed to "prepare" to have these behavior patterns, or defects, removed from my normal way of reacting to life's situations. I learned that this preparation was the essence of Step Six.

One of my patterns consisted of needing to be in control of just about everything in my life—finances, work, people, and pets! After being able to identify this behavior I knew that I wanted to get rid of it. But at the same time, I knew that there were valid reasons for my need to be in control. I had suffered some abuse during my drinking period that left me with fear of the same events being repeated in my sobriety. This was an unreasonable fear, and it caused me difficulty. My response to this fear was to need to control everyone and everything around me. I came to understand that it was this type of leftover damage from my past that could cause a relapse. I had come to rely on this control as a way of protecting myself. Yet the opposite was true. My need to control was actually causing me harm. I was helped to understand that I could use this step and this process to find a way to get rid of this defect. I had been under the false impression that my control was an asset, so it was difficult to think about relinquishing it. I learned that I can only control my own actions and that I have no control over the actions of other people. This insight, as well as other similar revelations, helped me to understand the purpose and value of Step Six. My mentors told me that Step Six was the preparation step for finding a way to be free from the need to control my life, and that this is where I had to seek to change my attitude about holding onto this false protection. I did not have to ask for its removal until Step Seven. I only had to find the willingness to have it removed.

My resistance to the process of preparation for this type of effort was characteristic of my personality. I never liked to prepare for anything in my life. I did not enjoy practicing for basketball games as a young person; I just wanted to play the game and compete. I did not want to take driving lessons; I just wanted to be able to pass my driver's test and get behind the wheel of my parents' car. As an adult, I had not changed very much. I still wanted to arrive at my destination without ever taking the trip to get there, whether in sports, education, or my career. Yet when I came to understand some of the defects that were causing me pain, I wanted to be rid of them. So I tried to proceed with Step Six.

My mentors also reminded me that I would never be able to work any of these steps to perfection. The preparation did not involve the actual asking for the removal of any of my defects—just to be ready to have them removed. The Step Six key words are "entirely ready." It is obvious to anyone that this is not humanly possible. No one is able to be *entirely ready* to have their each and every defect removed. So this step is based on a change in attitude. As it states in the *Twelve and Twelve* text, "Step Six . . . is A.A.'s way of stating the best possible attitude one can take in order to make a beginning on this lifetime job."[7] And although it is not a step that can be worked to perfection, it *is* a step that needs to be worked to the best of our ability. I had to make an attempt at this step. I needed to make a start. I was able to offer my willingness to get rid of the defects that made me uncomfortable, and then I had to try to offer my willingness to get rid the defects that I did not want to surrender. I had to ask God to help me find the willingness to let go of these.

I did become willing to have God help me remove my obsessive control. I was told that if God could remove my desire and obsession to drink, he could handle any other defect that I was willing to present to Him. My trust in the God of my understanding increased the longer I was able to stay sober. My trust in the people who had gone before me and their wisdom also grew stronger. This trust translated into willingness to try to be ready to have my defects removed.

I now understand much more about this step and how it works. I know that I could not have seen all of my defects at one time, and this was a gift.

I would have been overwhelmed with my own truth if I had had that insight or understanding early in my sobriety. My most destructive defects were contained in my inventory, and these were the ones that were of the most danger to my sobriety. They had to be dealt with as soon as I understood their nature and how they affected me and others. Over time I became aware of other defects as I listened and learned. I eventually started seeing a therapist who helped me immensely as I came to understand the nature of my defects and how they impacted my life. This was very important to my attitude of readiness for having them removed.

As I looked back over my early recovery years I realized that there were many times when I was focused on one or a few of my defects of character, trying to make changes, when God was at work in another area of my life without my awareness. I was growing and changing—and it was happening by God's grace. I truly believe that this is because of the willingness that I had acquired in doing the preparation in Step Six. I was reaping the benefits of sober living!

STEP SIX FOR EVERYONE

Ultimately Step Six is about the building of character. It is usually easy for any of us to understand why we would want to be free from the obsessive behavior that we claimed in Step One, whether it is compulsive gambling, spending, overeating, or working. When the glaring and inappropriate activities stop after we surrender our obsession to the God of our understanding, it is natural to want to sit back and relax as we enjoy the freedom we receive from the release of the guilt and shame associated with these behaviors. But then we discover that, in order to maintain this freedom, we need to remove other character flaws.

All spiritual growth requires the willingness to have our defects of character removed. All human instinct opposes this proposition. Therefore, all of us need to seek the willingness required to engage in this process.

> I do not understand the mystery of grace—only that it meets us where we are, but does not leave us where it found us.
> ~Anne LaMott

When I was growing up, the message that I heard in my church was that I was a sinner and that I needed God's grace to forgive me before I could find salvation, peace, or happiness. The message that I found in the Twelve Steps was reversed. I found that God loves us unconditionally, and that it is because of this unconditional love and grace that I have the strength and courage to look at myself with rigorous honesty, to identify my sin or character defects. It might seem that the message is the same since both proclaim that we are loved unconditionally and that we have character defects or sins. Yet for me it made a world of difference to understand the unconditional love before I was able to look below the surface at my faults.

> It's the action, not the fruit of the action, that's important. You have to do the right thing. It may not be in your power, may not be in your time, that there'll be any fruit. But that doesn't mean you stop doing the right thing. You may never know what results come from your action. But if you do nothing, there will be no result.
> —*Gandhi*

There is a wonderful book by Philip Yancey called *What's So Amazing About Grace?* [8]. In this book Yancey states that the church has been proclaiming the message of God's love in a way that does not invite people to join the church. He states the same truth that I discovered in my own spiritual journey with the Twelve Steps. He points out that the church tries to lure people to join by convincing them that they are bad because they were created as sinners, and therefore can only find relief from this terrible human condition by coming to church and finding the grace of God. Much of this theology is based on the second creation story in the Bible—the story of Adam and Eve—found in the book of Genesis. Adam and Eve were created and were told by God not to eat from the Tree of Life. When they disobeyed God in the Garden of Eden, sin entered the world. Hence, the belief that people were created as 'sinners' emerged as a common interpretation of this story, and became a tenet of Christian theology over the years. Yancey goes on to talk about the fact that we have lost touch with the first creation story in Genesis. In this account the story is described as taking place in seven days, when God created earth and mankind. After each day God looks at what He has done and states that it is good. On the last day when God creates man, He looks at him and says that this is *very good.* The difference between these two approaches to creation is phenomenal. The first story states that God created us as something that is very good, and therefore, this is the foundation of who we are. We are created in His image, and this is a good thing, not a bad thing. No, we are certainly not without sin.

But the fact that we are very good in the eyes of God is a fabulous way of approaching Step Six. We are given an opportunity to try to be ready to have God remove the stumbling blocks that stand in the way of our being able to enjoy the creation that we were given at our birth.

The Twelve Steps offers a different approach from the message delivered in a typical Christian church. It offers the concept that first we recognize that we are not able to handle life on our own power, that there is at least one thing that we are powerless over. After we acknowledge our powerlessness, then we can be open to the power of a God of our understanding. Once we establish this relationship with this Higher Power, we can then turn to seek the truth about our own human condition. It is the grace of this Higher Power that enables this process to evolve in our lives. Once we identify the behavior that has caused us difficulty and often harmed others, we are able to turn back to this same Power to begin to seek the true nature of who we were created to be.

To find the "original creation" of ourselves, we need to be able to strip away the negative and harmful behavior that distorts our native character. We cannot do this by our own unaided will. We need to seek God's help when the willingness is not within us. We need to find a state of readiness to ask God with humility to remove these barriers to our true self.

THE MYSTERY REVEALED IN THE SIMPLICITY OF STEP SIX

> Preparation to have our defects of character removed is a process where we gain something we need rather than losing something that we thought we wanted.

When first approaching Step Six, it can easily appear to the casual observer that this step is about God. The simple fact of this step is that by being ready, by preparing to have our defects of character removed by God, it is about us. We think we are getting ready to let go and give up something we treasure—our defects that we thought made us feel good or served some other positive purpose. Yet the truth is that by getting ready we are gaining something. We are gaining character and strength in our sobriety, freedom from obsessive behavior, and a deeper relationship with the God of our understanding. We are the ones who benefit by seeking the willingness to move forward.

STEP SIX

SELF-STUDY QUESTIONS

1. What is your definition of the word *character*? Why is it important to have good character?

2. What objections do you have, if any, to becoming ready to have God remove your defects? If you have no objections, then describe why you are comfortable with beginning this step.

3. Have you decided what defects of character you need to have removed? If not, go back to your Fourth Step inventory and try to find the underlying defects that caused your wrongdoings. If you are still baffled, seek someone to help you to review your inventory to begin to identify your character defects.

4. What are your expectations of completing this step?

Chapter 7

EMBRACING HUMILITY

STEP SEVEN

HUMBLY ASKED HIM TO REMOVE OUR SHORTCOMINGS

Step Six was about changing my attitude, and Step Seven is back to action, where I was to seek to change my behavior. I was now ready to engage in an exercise that required me to ask for God's grace in removing those parts of my character that were standing in my way of true freedom.

I have come to understand that beginning this step was only possible after working Step Six, where I had intentionally focused on acquiring the willingness to have my defects removed. It was incredible how I kept seeing the infinite wisdom in not only the concepts and contents of the steps, but also in the order of the steps. There is universal truth throughout the entire process of working this program.

Without the willingness that I received through my Step Six work, my approach to having my shortcomings removed was still self-centered and more like a demand than a request. I wanted my defects to be removed so that I would feel better and be happy. I was not at all focused on the first and most important word in this step—*humbly*. I was supposed to ask *humbly* for my shortcomings to be removed—not to demand that they be removed. And the defects were not necessarily to be the ones that

> Be yourself. Everyone else is taken.
> —*Oscar Wilde*

I wanted to have removed because they caused me discomfort. I was to focus on asking God to remove *all* of my defects, as stated in Step Six.

As with the previous steps, it took a certain amount of time in sobriety before I could come to understand this step. When I would meet with my mentors and listen to them talk, often the subject of the meeting would be humility. I would hear them talk about how all of them had suffered great humiliations as a result of their alcoholic drinking. But they explained that there is a great difference between humiliation and humility. I ultimately came to understand this for myself. Humiliation comes as a result of some behavior that is blatantly wrong and displayed in a public setting so that others know of your failing. It hurts to face people after a humiliating experience. It is embarrassing and degrading and it often induces guilt and shame. Humility is really the flip side of humiliation. Humility is about putting God and God's will as a priority and as the focus of our actions. Humility is something we seek when making major life decisions. The following statement from the *Twelve and Twelve* summarizes this concept that I learned:

> As long as we placed self-reliance first, a genuine reliance upon a Higher Power was out of the question. That basic ingredient of all humility, a desire to seek and do God's will, was missing.[9]

In conjunction with learning that humility is about putting God first, I also came to understand that humility is about seeking to be the person God created me to be. This has become a great comfort to me. I now know that by seeking to have my defects of character and my shortcomings removed from my life, I am gaining in the freedom to be myself. It is only when I get close to this objective that I will ever find freedom. As long as I try to be something or someone I am not meant to be, I will be a failure at my attempts at finding true happiness and joy. When I first got sober and had been released from the obsession to drink, I wanted to "be" my mentor. I did not want to be "like" her—I wanted to "be" her. I tried to copy her in how I talked about the steps, whom I chose to have for friends, what meetings I attended, and how I dressed. I did not know exactly what I could do to "be" her, but I tried my best in whatever way made sense to me. Obviously, I failed! It was only when I started to accept that it was okay to be who I really was with all of my own skills, talents, and appearance that I was able to begin to experience any kind of peace of mind. This was a freedom that I never dreamed of experiencing in my life. I had always suffered from low self-esteem, feeling unaccepted by others and unacceptable to myself. This acceptance of who I was created to be did not happen quickly, but it did happen gradually after repeatedly practicing all of the principles of the Twelve Steps. Step Seven was an integral part of this process as I worked at discovering the strength of my own character.

I had to learn that this step was not about my agenda. Just as I had discovered during my work with Step Six in trying to become ready to have my defects removed, I found that often I would be focusing on seeking help with a particular character defect while God was busy helping me to remove another one that I was not working on at the time. For example, I remember struggling with the fear of being alone and living by myself. As I continued to seek freedom from this fear, God was busy with preparing to help me to remove my extreme self-centeredness. I was not consciously asking for help with my self-centeredness; although this was a defect that I saw clearly during my work on Step Four. Just as I became comfortable with living alone, He sent someone to me who needed a place to live. I had an extra room, and she moved in.

These events all took place after I started to work on Steps Six and Seven. I thought that I could focus on one defect at a time. But the reality was that character defects, shortcomings, or sins—whatever word is used to describe these traits—are not isolated entities that can be neatly eliminated from our lives as if they are something that can be removed through surgery. As I was trying to focus on my fear of being alone, God was opening a door to show me a glimpse of my self-centeredness. I wanted to be comfortable being alone, or live with someone who would be a life partner. Instead of just removing my fear, I was given an opportunity to learn how to live with someone who had needs that I could help satisfy by sharing my home. I did not want to do this because it meant that I would need to be attentive to another person's circumstances. It would not be about my needs, but about her needs. A lesson that I learned from this life changing experience was that as I did not get rid of 100 percent of my fear, and I did not get rid of all of my self-centeredness. But I did make progress in each of these areas of my life. I discovered that there was progress with my defects, and that I could expect to continue to make progress with these defects and all of my other defects. But they would never be entirely removed.

Ultimately, I came to believe that there are two primary reasons for my defects not being entirely removed. First, if I ever became entirely free from all of my defects, I would no longer need God in my life. I would be perfect! Of course, this would never happen. Second, many of my defects are really natural instincts that are God-given and necessary for life. These instincts become defects when I misuse them and let them control me. For example, fear is an emotion that played havoc in my life. Yet I need to be fearful when I face a legitimate danger.

During my heavy drinking I had a horrible fear of heights and of being alone in any building at any time of day, including my house. I feared that I would be attacked and would be killed. I soon became free from this type of fear. But sometimes fear is a necessary instinct that provides us motivation to seek protection. If I had no fear of driving faster than my car allows for safety, I would be a danger to myself or others. If I had no fear of strangers kidnapping children, I would have not been a protective mother to my son and daughter. Fear, as well as anger, is necessary when danger lurks. Irrational fear, though, is paralyzing and needs to be removed.

It was important for me to try to understand the process I was encountering when having my defects removed. It was important that I not feel as if I were failing at this phase of my recovery. *Defects do not disappear overnight.* I soon realized that God often uses others or outside circumstances to help us change our old habits. We can seek direction and help from professionals as well as mentors who have experience with the Twelve Steps. The important thing to remember is to be persistent with our humble request to have them removed, and always to be willing to have them removed with God's help. It is potentially dangerous for us only when we resist giving up a defect or say that we refuse to give up a defect.

Something else we should be aware of is that we might suffer through a grieving process with the removal of some of our defects, as we did when we admitted our powerlessness over alcohol and asked that the obsession to drink be removed from our life. Feeling grief does not mean that we have done something wrong or that there is any kind of problem. This is a natural response. The grief is similar to the process in Step One of coming to acceptance of powerlessness and unmanageability.

The process we use to humbly ask God to remove our defects is not important. We must do whatever works for us as individuals. I started my process by using the prayer found in *Alcoholics Anonymous* that is suggested for this step:

> My creator, I am now willing that you should have all of me, good and bad. I pray that you now remove from me every single defect of character which stands in the way of my usefulness to you and my fellows. Grant me strength, as I go out from here, to do your bidding. Amen.[10]

Willingness and humility are powerful attributes that empower the character-changing possibilities of Steps Six and Seven. Although the intent was for me to become useful to God and to my fellows, I was the ultimate benefactor of these steps.

STEP SEVEN FOR EVERYONE

Step Seven invites anyone who is willing to grow spiritually into one of many spiritual practices of self-discipline required on this journey. This is a step that requires courage and fortitude. It is also a step that leads to an amazing inner peace and tranquility. The process of seeking God's help in removing our character defects can look like another time of defeat—a time when we are giving up on ourselves and our own capabilities. Yet the opposite is true. This is a time when we find ourselves and gain strength to pursue the next part of our recovery, where we reconcile ourselves to those whom we have caused harm. It is a time when humility becomes something we want to embrace in our lives.

This practice of seeking to grow spiritually by developing our character is not unique to the fellowship of Alcoholics Anonymous. It is not even unique to religious communities. I was blessed to be part of an education community that was also very focused on building character. My son attended a private boarding school that was based on the principles of character building. As part of the foundation of the schools program, the students were given two grades for each class they attended—one for their academic achievement and one for character achievement. It was an amazing school! The students were taught to live their lives based on truth, integrity, and courage. They were taught that character was just as important as knowledge.

The parents were also involved in the school in a unique way. Because students were enrolled from across the nation, the parents were assigned to parent groups that were located in the region where they lived, and the groups met once a month. Basically, the parents were asked to do work that was similar to what their children were asked to do, based on the concept that the environment raising the child would have to change in order for the student to maintain the life-changing character traits he or she was expected to adopt. The old adage of "the apple doesn't fall far from the tree" was used in many sessions. This meant that without change in the family, students would have a more difficult time in maintaining the change that was happening in their lives.

I was confronted at my very first parent meeting with an exercise that was similar to my early encounters with folks from Alcoholics Anonymous. We were put into small groups of six parents, and the first thing we had to do was describe who we were without using any titles. I could not say that I was a mother or manager. I actually remember crying as I opened up and tried to share the honest appraisal of my own personhood because at the time I was involved in counseling and was struggling with issues that surfaced during my divorce. A principle that was one of the building blocks of this program was "When in doubt, bet on the truth." The truth of who I am can often be scary, and something that I want to run from—or at least ignore. But here was a group of people who were similar to my sober friends, people who were living their lives in a way that demanded honest self-appraisal and seeking to build character through humility. It was outstanding to understand that these values are really universal. What I experienced during my son's two years in this school prior to his graduation was transforming—for myself, my son, my family, and many other families. I saw young people find a way of life that would become a solid foundation for living. Lives of families were changed and relationships were healed between parent and child. This all happened years ago now, and my son has grown into an amazing young man with a foundation for life that is based on character.

I have seen this same type of transformation whenever humility and character are sought through many other programs. I have seen it in the Christian church, the Hindu religion, the Hyde School where my son attended, as well as the fellowship of Alcoholics Anonymous and the Twelve Steps,. In each of these endeavors, it was always achieved by asking for help from some higher power. I learned in my sobriety that some people used the group as their higher power. For me, it was with the God of my understanding. I have never known this transformation process to fail for anyone who chose to pursue growth by using the principles of this program.

THE MYSTERY REVEALED IN THE SIMPLICITY OF STEP SEVEN

> **When we surrender our defects of character, we discover the person we were created to be.**

Humility is not negative, it is positive. The mystery in Step Seven is similar to the mystery discovered in Step One where we need to surrender our control over our addictive or obsessive behavior. Admitting powerlessness and humbly asking for the removal of our shortcomings, sins, or character defects is strength, not weakness. In Step Seven, we find the strength in the new character that emerges as we become the person God has created us to be. The weakness is in continuing to try to change ourselves using our own strength and our own willpower. Typically, this is a "clenched teeth" approach in our attempts to rid ourselves of these problem behaviors or attitudes. With Step Seven, serenity and peace are the result of exercising humility.

In Response to the Steps

STEP SEVEN

SELF-STUDY QUESTIONS

1. What is your definition of humility?

2. List examples of the defects that you are asking God to remove from your life.

3. What character traits do you value and want to grow in your life?

4. How are you being held accountable to working Step Seven?

Chapter 8

PREPARING FOR AMENDS

STEP EIGHT

MADE A LIST OF ALL PERSONS WE HAD HARMED, AND BECAME WILLING TO MAKE AMENDS

When I first looked at Step Eight, I thought that this would be a simple task to complete. But I learned a very important lesson early in my sobriety that served me in good stead with this step. I heard people talk about not jumping into this process too quickly. They shared their experience with this step and Step Nine, where amends are made to those who were harmed by the destructive behavior of their disease. Many people quickly jumped into these two steps, and in fact often skipped this one entirely. They really did not think that making a list was important since they already knew whom they had hurt—especially family members they were either living with or who had separated themselves from the alcoholic. They wanted to move fast and make restitution.

> I have never been especially impressed by the heroics of people convinced that they are about to change the world; I am more awed by those who struggle to make one small difference after another.
> ~Ellen Goodman

The reality was that they did move fast but did not accomplish the goal of these two steps. These folks came to understand that they were acting quickly often because of their own guilt and shame. They wanted to be freed from this, and they wanted to feel good. They understood that they had caused legitimate harm to others, but they had not laid the foundation for approaching their amends with the proper attitude and the ability to truly amend their behavior. The previous discussion on the steps validates that much work has to be accomplished in order to approach Steps Eight and Nine with a clear understanding of the purpose of making the list and the details of the amends. Just saying "I'm sorry" is not sufficient!

I don't mean to imply that Step Eight is complex. It is not. But it does need to be done intentionally and with time set aside to focus on the content of the list. I chose to go on a retreat to provide a quiet space where I would be able to think about the list without interruptions from my daily routine. I was also approaching my first marriage and wanted to "clean house" prior to beginning that new relationship. I made sure to take my Fourth Step inventory with me because I wanted to use the details as a base for writing the list of those persons whom I had caused harm.

I had a separate notebook to use for my list. I began my efforts at this important work with the third-step prayer. I definitely wanted to be freed from the bondage of myself as I tried to do an honest appraisal for this list. As I wrote down the name of a person, I also took the time to write a description of exactly what actions I had done that had caused harm to this individual. I was very intent on being thorough with my list, so I did not limit it just to events that surrounded my drinking. I tried to go back to my childhood and work my way through my whole life. It was important to list not only those things that I had done that had caused harm but also the things that I did not do that I should have done. An example of this would be the lack of communication and visits with my parents during the years of my heavy drinking. Another example was the poor performance I had done in each of my jobs as a result of not being mentally available much of the time that I was employed during my drinking. I certainly did not perform up to my best capabilities during that time.

The result of the experience of creating my list was an overwhelming awareness of the depth of my disease of alcoholism. I came to understand that this disease had permeated every area of my life and affected my mind, body, and spirit. It was a disease that did not reside in a bottle; it could not be measured by how much I drank or when I drank. I had a new appreciation for the total destructiveness of this disease to my physical health and every relationship in my life—family, friends, and even acquaintances. I was grateful for this insight, which led me to an even deeper commitment to maintaining my sobriety. I did not want to be a person who created this type of carnage in the world. Before making this list, I certainly had knowledge of the wrongs that I had done, but I did not appreciate my own ability to affect so many others.

Going through this list immediately enabled me to grasp the last part of the step. I was once again confronted with the concept of willingness and having to acquire the willingness this time to make amends to all of the people on my list. The separation of preparing before taking action was once again introduced into the flow of the steps with Step Eight and Step Nine. It was important for me once again to be intentional in acknowledging this separation prior to making the list so I would not be tempted to leave off names of people I did not want to deal with in Step Nine. I truly did ignore the issue of one day needing to speak with the people on the list. There were several I did not relish approaching, either because of my own fear of what they might say or because I wanted to justify my behavior as a reaction to something they had done that had harmed me. I know today that because I approached this step with prayer and a time of retreat, I was able to be thorough with the names I listed. I did not skip over any that I was aware of, even if I was uncomfortable considering some of the people on my list.

After approaching the step as I had, it was not difficult for me to find the willingness to make amends. I am convinced that my understanding of my disease moved to a new level when I was able to be honest to the point of recognizing the total depth of the disease. I wanted desperately never to repeat this level of harm to anyone, but especially to those I loved. So I was able to say that I was willing to make amends. It would be up to my mentors to help with the process of actually making the amends when I began my ninth step. That was to come later.

STEP EIGHT FOR EVERYONE

Someone pointed out to me a most unlikely place to find a reference to the fourth and eighth steps of Alcoholics Anonymous. The following quotation is taken from the novel *Payment in Kind* by J.A. Jance.

> Anyone who thinks the Alcoholics Anonymous program is a walk in the park hasn't sat down to do Step 4, which entails making a searching moral inventory of yourself, or Step 8, which involves making a list of all the people you have wronged in your life-time, people to whom you ought to make amends while you still have a chance.[11]

It was exciting to find this reference outside of the familiar literature of the AA program. The process of making a list of people we have harmed is not typically something that people are taught to do when they grow up. It might come as a result of engaging in therapy or certain spiritual disciplines.

It is odd that mankind has not accepted the wisdom of the spiritual giants who uncovered this astounding truth about living a life of peace and serenity: the wisdom that says we cannot have peace and serenity without establishing and maintaining right relationships with people in our lives. Right relationships are critical to our achieving this desired mental and spiritual state of being.

People in recovery from the disease of alcoholism are highly motivated to restore their broken relationships. The damage caused by the disease is usually obvious and detailed in the moral inventory. This step is even more difficult for those who have damaged relationships that are not as obvious and visible. It is usually easy to identify the harm from drugs and alcohol, but it is more difficult to create the list of people we have harmed through overeating or workaholism. We all have inflicted some type of harm on others, and most often those we love. Workaholics often neglect quality time with family under the guise of needing to provide income. Overeaters think that harm is only caused to themselves through their overweight, yet what about those who love them? The health risks associated with being overweight can cause great pain if the extra weight causes ill health. What about those who are addicted to smoking and the second-hand smoke that affects those around them? What about the possible health issues that can result in their sickness or death, ultimately leaving their loved ones with great grief to bear? Step Eight is the beginning of the process for healing these hurts and living in as much harmony as possible. This is the final preparation step for removing any guilt or shame that we carry from our past.

It is important to keep in mind that making this list is a *preparation* for the amends that need to be made. It is especially important when we also need to add the names of people who have harmed us. It is difficult to remain objective when thinking of our own hurts. When this thinking interferes with our ability to add a name to our list, then we must once again resort to the third-step prayer and ask God to remove us from the bondage of self. This prayer has never failed to give me strength and courage when confronted with a difficult task that I need to accomplish to help me to grow spiritually.

If we shortchange ourselves with this process, then it is like putting a Band-Aid on a wound that needs surgery. Even if the wound appears to be healed on the surface, it is not healed internally. Shortchanging ourselves by skipping over making this list does not result in anything but additional resentment, pain, or guilt that will block our own happiness.

The final part of this step—"and became willing to make amends to them all"—is just as important as the list. Once again, the third-step prayer is the key to acquiring the willingness for preparation for Step Nine. Courage is the final ingredient required for moving on to the ninth step—courage to continue with the final phase of building this foundation for a new life.

THE MYSTERY REVEALED IN THE SIMPLICITY OF STEP EIGHT

> **The process for eliminating the list of people we have harmed starts with creating the list.**

We have a list of people we have harmed, whether we acknowledge it or not. The only way to eliminate the list is by creating the list. The mystery is simply that we need to create a list to remove the list from our hearts and minds.

STEP EIGHT

SELF-STUDY QUESTIONS

1. What process will you use to compose your list of people you have harmed?

2. Discuss your list with someone you trust. Have them help you to make sure that you have included all family members, past and present; all business acquaintances and creditors; all those who are no long available because of your location or their death.

3. Review what you have done to become willing to make these amends in Step Nine? Are you willing to make amends to all the people on your list?

4. Are you willing to set a date for completing this process? If so, share the date with someone who will hold you accountable. If not, journal about why you are not willing to commit to a completion date.

Chapter 9

SEEKING FORGIVENESS

STEP NINE

MADE DIRECT AMENDS TO SUCH PEOPLE WHEREVER POSSIBLE, EXCEPT WHEN TO DO SO WOULD INJURE THEM OR OTHERS

One of my favorite sentimental movies is *Love Story*, starring Ryan O'Neal and Ali MacGraw. The one line from the movie that caught my attention, along with that of millions of other Americans, was, "Love means never having to say you're sorry." I saw this film in the midst of my "drinking career" and was totally swept away with the romanticism of the story as well as the concept of never having to be sorry (which was *my* interpretation of that phrase). I barely remember the details of the story after all of these years, but I have always remembered that line.

As I continued to work on my sobriety and my new way of life, I quickly came to understand that Step Nine embodied the opposite concept from this movie one-liner. This attractive phrase that caught on with my generation implied that it was possible to find a love so deep that it would be unconditional. We were led to believe that there was no wrong that could not be understood or accepted. Of course, this is not a sound spiritual axiom. It is not possible for human beings to love unconditionally, even though we seek to find that in marriage and partnered relationships. We all cause hurt to others because we are human, and we need to be accountable for our actions and when possible make restitution for any harm that we cause.

Step Nine was explained to me as a step that should be taken with great care and under consultation with a mentor who could guide me. The literature from Alcoholics Anonymous states that there are three primary qualities required for approaching the work to be done with this step—timing, courage, and prudence.[12] It also suggests that this work be done in consultation with someone with experience.

I began by sitting with my mentor and reviewing the list that I had completed on my retreat. In reviewing the list, my mentor asked me questions about the harm that I had caused those people I had listed. After sharing my honest appraisal of myself and the people I had harmed, I began to recognize patterns of behavior. I found new information that I had not been able to understand during my Fourth Step. During this conversation, my mentor encouraged me and gave me hope that I would be able to have right relationships with family and friends if I would be courageous enough to pursue direct amends with these people. One of the patterns that I identified was how I had always relied on others to make me happy and to make me feel accepted. I came to understand that this type of pattern would always result in faulty dependence that would ultimately destroy any meaningful relationship. The type of acceptance and love that I was seeking was similar to what I had witnessed in *Love Story*. I was struggling to understand that the only unconditional love that would ever be possible would come from my Higher Power. The acceptance that I sought was beginning to emerge through my efforts at working these steps. The final piece to the foundation for a successful life of love and acceptance was to make amends to those I had harmed and to restore the key relationships in my life to a healthy status.

After this insightful consultation with my mentor, I was ready to move forward with making my amends. When I made the commitment to start this process, I knew that the timing was right. The timing was simply based on the completion of the first eight steps. I had done them as thoroughly as possible with the help of the people in the program and with the grace of God. Great guidance from those with the wisdom of their own experience and strength helped me to be rigorous in my own efforts at working these steps to the best of my ability. The God of my understanding honored these efforts and prepared me for being able to make amends.

One key concept to understand as I approached this important work was the true meaning of the word *amend*. Amend means *to change*. It does not mean simply saying, "I'm sorry" or "please forgive me." Making amends is about change, and without changed behavior, the spoken words of the amend is meaningless. Without change, those we approach will not trust in our sincerity if they experience no difference in our actions. This is why Steps Six and Seven are so critical to the success of Step Nine. By the time I was approaching my amends, I had already changed a lot of my destructive behavior. I was becoming a person who could be trusted.

This process revealed another affirmation of how the steps are truly inspired and how the process is flawless. The goal of Step Nine is to seek forgiveness for the harm we have caused; yet how difficult would it be for those we are approaching if they see that we are still repeating the same wrong behaviors. How can the sincerity of our words seeking forgiveness be honored and accepted if we are still behaving in the same harmful ways? By working on Steps Six and Seven, we engage in the process of amending our lives through the changes that result from our willingness to have God remove our defects of character.

Another lesson I learned from listening to others is that the purpose of making the amends was not to help me feel better. There would be times and circumstances when I approached some of the people on my list who were still angry with me and who would not be willing to forgive me. I was told that if I experienced this type of response, it was okay. I had not failed at working the step. Step Nine is about my actions of seeking forgiveness. The success of the step is not dependent in any way on the results of my actions. I needed to be focused on my own housecleaning through my efforts at these amends. I also needed to have the support of others who had experience with this step, because if I was rejected in any way during this process, I could go to them to talk about what happened. I could use them to remind me that the process of direct amends was for me to change and seek forgiveness, not about my receiving forgiveness. Those who are unable to forgive are the ones who suffer the most, because they are the ones who will live with resentments and continue to be in bondage to negative energy.

> Many promising reconciliations have broken down because, while both parties come to forgive, neither party comes to be forgiven.
> ~Charles Williams

Although the previous steps required courage, I found that Step Nine required the most courage. This is where I stepped out from my comfort zone. When working the other steps, I was surrounded with acceptance for all of my efforts. I was uplifted with hope and encouraged by others who had faith in my ability to stay sober and change my life. This step was requiring me to go to people who did not understand the steps, and most likely would not understand the process of this specific step. I had experienced a lot of resistance from others who did not think that I even had a problem with my drinking; they thought my behaviors were okay because often they were just like me. My disease did not seek to spend time with sober people; it sought to spend time with people who had the same life style as mine. So, there was a strong possibility that my meetings with them would not be well received, and I needed to be prepared for this possibility.

One of the defects I understood about myself was my fear of being rejected. I had certainly asked God to remove this fear, but even after three years of sobriety, it was not totally removed. I discovered that for making my amends to certain people on my list, I needed to find courage that would overcome this fear. It was at this point in my recovery that I was once again reminded to think about why I was attempting to do this difficult task. I was doing it simply to stay sober. I was not attempting to become a "good person" or achieve any other altruistic goal. When fear blocked my courage to make an appointment to speak with someone, or when fear consumed me before talking with the person, I thought back to my first-step inventory and remembered how desperate I was when I first got sober. I was coached to think about these things so that I would find the courage to continue with my purpose. This worked for me, and I was able to share with the people on my list my reasons for seeking their forgiveness. I was able to share that I was working this program of recovery, and that I understood I needed to make restitution for harm done. I then asked for their forgiveness.

There were varied responses. Most were gracious, some were hurtful. But after each encounter, I left with the knowledge that I had honored myself by being willing to tackle my own fear and stand on the faith of the fellowship of people who had worked these steps. I believed that they knew this difficult work would result in my own ability to stay sober. This belief has been greatly rewarded. I have wonderful relationships with everyone in my family, and I have strong and beautiful friendships that are rooted in honesty and integrity. Most importantly, I have also been able to maintain continuous sobriety.

The final quality cited in the literature was prudence. Prudence was critical to this process and was related to the last phrase of the step: "except when to do so would injure them or others." It was important that I not cause further harm to any individual as a result of my working these amends for my own benefit. Simply stated, I could not reveal information to someone that would hurt them, or that they could use to harm another individual. During the conversation with my mentor when I reviewed my list, I was able to address the prudence of each one and confirm which amends were valid and would not cause any further damage.

When I had completed Step Nine, I had a wonderful sense of satisfaction. For the first time in my life, I felt that I was standing on solid ground because I had right relationships with God, myself, and the people in my life.

STEP NINE FOR EVERYONE

Seeking forgiveness is a common theme in many faith traditions. Most often it is presented to us in terms of seeking forgiveness from God and having the assurance that we have that forgiveness. The faith traditions also present the concept of forgiving others as a key ingredient to spiritual wholeness and growth. And finally, the concept of seeking forgiveness from others is also included as something that we need to do to for maintaining right relationships.

Jan G.

It is easy to think that we only need to approach God and seek forgiveness from Him rather than also seeking forgiveness from those we have harmed. But if we are attempting to restore broken relationships, then we must remember that this is a twofold process. First, we seek their forgiveness through a direct face-to-face meeting, or through a written document of some kind. But second, we need to continue to work the steps to make sure that we work on our character defects so that our lives are truly amended and changed, and that we do not repeat the same harmful actions.

The motivator for all of us to do the hard work required in this step is still Step One, where we identify our powerlessness and unmanageability with whatever addiction or problem we identified. We continue to seek to understand the compulsive or addictive behavior that we are addressing in our lives and to find patterns of behavior from our Step Eight list.

For those who are seeking to grow spiritually and have not identified any addictive behaviors, this is still extremely appropriate and necessary. Our spiritual health is directly linked to our human relationships. When we have broken relationships or unreconciled harm in our lives, we will have a tainted relationship with the God of our understanding. Unresolved damage to others causes shame and guilt that can block our inner peace and contentment. It is especially damaging to our self-image when we are in touch with our past wrongs and have not made amends to those we have hurt.

A spiritual director or therapist can help with discerning the process for making amends and the content of our apologies. It is especially important to remember to include those who have died. A suggested way to handle these amends is to write a letter to these individuals or to offer some community service as an effort to offer restitution.

The rewards of Step Nine are available to any who choose to engage in this process. The only requirement is the courage to be willing to seek reconciliation in a personal and direct conversation for any harm we have caused for others.

THE MYSTERY REVEALED IN THE SIMPLICITY OF STEP NINE

> **It could appear that talking opens old wounds, yet it is only through talking and seeking forgiveness that we find the closure that is needed for healing.**

We are meant to live in a right relationship with God and our fellow human beings. The human condition dictates that we will not be able to do this without causing harm to others along the way. The Step Nine process of making amends offers a way to correct broken relationships. The natural response to our wrongdoings is to try to forget about them and hope that others will also forget about any harm we have caused. The reality is that harm festers and continues to poison the relationship until it is reconciled. The only way to avoid lingering resentments is to address them directly. This admission of our wrongdoing is the way to positive and healthy relationships. It could appear that talking opens old wounds, yet it is only through talking and seeking forgiveness that we find the closure that is needed for healing.

STEP NINE

SELF-STUDY QUESTIONS

1. Who have you reviewed your list with? What information did you discover about your patterns in relationships?

2. Discuss your list with someone you trust. Have this person help you to identify who should receive a direct amend with a face-to-face meeting or some type of formal communication, or an indirect amend when this person is not available to you. (An example of an indirect amend would be volunteering to visit an elderly person on a regular basis, if your parents are no longer living and you were trying to make restitution for not spending time with them when they were alive.) Make an appointment to have this meeting.

3. Describe your attitude towards making amends to those you have harmed. What do you expect to receive from this process?

4. Are there any amends that you are avoiding? If so, why? What can you do to move forward?

5. Record the results of some of your efforts at making amends. What did the people say? How did you feel after you were finished?

Chapter 10

GOING FORWARD

STEP TEN

CONTINUED TO TAKE PERSONAL INVENTORY AND WHEN WE WERE WRONG, PROMPTLY ADMITTED IT

One of my favorite phrases from my early sobriety was "eternal vigilance is the price of sobriety." Often this was referring to the fact that in order to stay sober we will have to be diligent about our practice of the program of Alcoholics Anonymous—including going to meetings; talking with sponsors; sharing our experience, strength, and hope; and practicing the Twelve Steps. It instilled in me the firm belief that I would need to acquire a new way of life in order to combat my disease of addiction.

I have come to trust in this wisdom of eternal vigilance, based upon many years of observation. I have observed who has been able to maintain sobriety and who has relapsed into the disease by picking up a drink. Some have returned to share the fact that life did not get better after resuming their drinking, that life did not even stay the same as it had been at the time when they stopped working the program. Rather, life returned to the same chaos that first made them seek help through the program of recovery, and usually it was worse. There is still no scientific evidence of what causes this disease or what

> Every man is a damn fool for at least five minutes every day. Wisdom consists in not exceeding the limit.
> ~Elbert Hubbard

constitutes its physical attributes. But Alcoholics Anonymous has been around for more than seventy years and has acquired wisdom through the collective history of those who have passed through its doors. The facts are clear, and the evidence is powerful: the changes experienced through the practice of the steps are at risk if one does not continue to live by their principles.

I was also cautioned not to fall into the trap of believing that because of my new-found life, I was cured or recovered. Using these words could introduce the concept into my brain that I would now be able to drink in safety. The experience of those who had done this type of research on their own disease by drinking again offered proof that there is no recovery from this disease, in terms of being able to "drink normally," no matter how one might try to define the concept of "normal drinking." Therefore, I would refer to myself as a "recovering alcoholic" to keep this key principle in my active consciousness. I was also told that I would have to continue to take action against this disease on a daily basis as I move forward with my life.

The action for maintaining my sobriety would be to find a way to embrace the first nine steps as a new way of life. The last three steps satisfy this need by offering "maintenance" practices that embody the intent, spirit, and core principles of living this new way of life for a recovering alcoholic.

I was able to see clearly that my recovery grew from developing a personal relationship with God, a healthy relationship with myself, and then solid and wholesome relationships with key people in my life whom I loved, worked with, or socialized with. The last three steps offered a way to keep these new relationships in good order. Step Ten provides a way for me to manage my relationships with others. Step Eleven addresses my relationship with myself and with God. Step Twelve calls me to action to share what I have experienced with others.

Step Ten offers me a way to make sure that I maintain right relationships with those around me by continuing to look at my own actions, and when I make a mistake or harm another person, to make restitution for that harm immediately. It is amazing that once I had come to understand the purpose of Step Nine and had success with making amends, I did not fear trying to incorporate this into my daily life. I have arrived at a place where I feel uncomfortable if I know that I have done something wrong and have not acknowledged it or made restitution for it.

In addition to taking a daily inventory of my wrongs, I also learned that I had to continue to try to recognize my old patterns of behavior that were still part of my immediate reactions to many life situations. I needed to know what my triggers were, or what things made me react impulsively. I was very aware of my self-centeredness, my fear of economic insecurity, and my old resentments.

In Response to the Steps

I needed professional help beyond those who were sharing their experience with this program, so I sought therapists throughout my recovery to help me unravel behavior patterns that I was not able to understand or alter on my own. The steps gave me the courage to be open to this professional help. As a result, I was able to continue to recognize things that I did that caused damage not only to others but also to myself.

Initially, I tried to make a daily inventory and a go on a yearly retreat. I put aside time at the end of my day to review the events of the day to understand where I might have done something that would need an apology or some form of reconciliation. In addition, I found that by attending meetings, sharing openly and honestly with my mentors, friends, and therapists, I was able to identify situations where I was wrong. It took time for me to understand that I was not always to blame for a broken relationship. I needed a wise and objective listener to help me assess situations that were causing me pain or discomfort.

> If you sit down at set of sun
> And count the acts that you have done,
> And, counting, find
> One self-denying deed, one word
> That eased the heart of him who heard,
> One glance most kind
> That fell like sunshine where it went—
> Then you may count that day well spent.
> ~George Eliot

Going away for a spiritual retreat was also very beneficial to give me some quiet time to reflect on my life and what was happening. After I had children, it became more difficult to make time for this type of reflection, but the experiences were invaluable when I was able to go away. I still treasure the opportunities to participate in this type of self-examination and personal growth.

The methods that are used for maintaining a current status of any unresolved wrongdoings are not as important as the timeliness of the restitution. Each of us responds to this principle of staying current with our inventory in a different manner. The key to this step is that we "promptly" admit it. For those of us trying to recover from alcoholism, it is repeated throughout the literature of Alcoholics Anonymous that pride will lead the way to a quick exit from sobriety. The ego that believes it can commit no wrong or that it is not important to seek forgiveness on a daily basis after completing a Ninth Step is an ego that will eventually assume it can control its drinking. How do we know this? Experience and evidence from the many folks who have proven it to be true.

Delay in admitting our wrongs allows time for our minds to misconstrue the details of the events of the day. It is easier to rationalize our behavior than to admit that we can make a mistake or retreat into some old behavior.

Jan G.

The purpose of this step is to keep the slate clean and to allow us to live without guilt or shame. It is the first of the three steps that solidify our future life of staying sober. step ten for everyone

Recovery from all addictions, as well as all spiritual growth, needs vigilance and perseverance. Recovery and growth can be compared to a garden. A garden left untended will grow weeds, and eventually the weeds will choke out the original plants. I have experienced this phenomenon more than once in my gardening life. This same principle applies to the journey with the Twelve Step program. Human nature tends towards self-centeredness and contentment with the status quo. Complacency tries to lure even the most devoted participant.

Our relationships in life are no different. Step Ten is about relationships with others as well as with ourselves; it is about taking responsibility for our actions. Going through an inventory process and admitting our wrongs is something we all need to do in order to sustain our mental and spiritual health. The key to keeping a garden alive and growing is to weed it. It is easier to remove weeds when they are small than when they grow larger and start choking the healthy plants.

It is easiest to see the "weeds" that have come into our life when our day is completed. Often, we know immediately when we have done something wrong that can cause harm, but it is best to stop and think before we act on our restitution. It is important to understand the situation before speaking too quickly. So, "sleeping on it" is sometimes a good idea. But prompt action for admitting our wrongdoing is the spirit and intent of this step. The longer we wait, the more difficult it can be to take action.

An important concept to remember in making amends is that we do not try to rationalize our behavior by pointing out someone's faults. It is counter productive to say something like, "When you did so and so, I got angry and yelled at you. I was wrong and I am sorry." The "you" word is a word to be used carefully, as it can often attach itself to blame. This kind of a statement can instill resentment and defensiveness in the person we are trying to make amends with. It is better just to begin with our own actions. "I am sorry that I got angry and yelled at you." The focus of these words is "I." It says we are taking responsibility for what we did wrong.

> Look at a day when you are supremely satisfied at the end. It's not a day when you lounge around doing nothing; it's when you've had everything to do, and you've done it.
> ~*Margaret Thatcher*

When we reflect at the end of the day, it is also a time to think about motives behind our actions. Sometimes we harm others in indirect ways that still require prompt action for an apology. It is also good to reflect on our day with a list of the defects of character that we are trying to surrender to God. We can ask for help to see where these defects might have been active. We can ask questions like, "Did I feel fear over my economic circumstances, and did I take any wrong action as a result?" "Did I have wrong dependencies on my family or friends with the false expectation of their protecting me?" "Did I exaggerate the truth to feel superior to another?" "Did I gossip about anyone?" "Did I have any negative attitudes that influenced my behavior?"

A scheduled time for retreat is also important. This is perhaps one of the most difficult actions to incorporate into our routine. My own experience suggests that I am the last person to schedule personal time for reflection and growth. It is definitely one of my weaknesses.

A retreat is a time to assess our progress with our relationships with God, with ourselves, and with others. It is a time to take inventory of our life and pause to look at the things that need to be done to tend to our spiritual gardens.

Over time, this practice of identifying our wrong actions and making restitution as quickly as possible becomes a comfortable way of life. In fact it becomes uncomfortable when we try to ignore a mistake and avoid setting the record straight.

THE MYSTERY REVEALED IN THE SIMPLICITY OF STEP TEN

> **It is easier to stay current with making amends than to procrastinate and delay.**

The mystery of Step Ten is that our inventory decreases if we do it on a daily basis. It becomes easier instead of harder. It takes less time and energy than when we ignore the inventory and find ourselves with a long list of amends. It is important to resist the temptation to procrastinate when we know that we have done something wrong. After making sure that we understand our motives and what was our responsibility for our actions, it is best to respond quickly.

STEP TEN

SELF-STUDY QUESTIONS

1. Make a list of things that you have done to cause harm to others, or mistakes that you have made today. Are there any patterns that you see in relation to your character defects that you have been asking God to remove? Continue making this list every day.

2. Create a list of questions that you can ask yourself at the end of the day to do a "spot check" inventory of your day.

3. Are there any lingering amends that you need to address with anyone? If so, list them.

4. Describe what it is like to try to do a daily inventory? What kind of difficulties do you have with the process?

5. Recall a time when you caused harm to another, were aware of your actions, and did not take prompt action to apologize. What happened? How did you feel? What happened to the relationship that you had with the other person? What happened to your relationship with yourself?

Chapter 11

FINDING POWER

STEP ELEVEN

SOUGHT THROUGH PRAYER AND MEDITATION TO IMPROVE OUR CONSCIOUS CONTACT WITH GOD AS WE UNDERSTOOD HIM, PRAYING ONLY FOR KNOWLEDGE OF GOD'S WILL FOR US AND THE POWER TO CARRY THAT OUT

Step Eleven is the second of the maintenance steps. Step Ten focused on our relationships with others, and this step returns us to our relationship with the God of our understanding. At the beginning of my sobriety, I learned about powerlessness over alcohol, and how my life was unmanageable. With Step Eleven, I came to understand that I could find power once again. This power would not come from within. This was the power that was afforded to me because of the relationship that I developed with my God. The power was always there; it was merely a process for me to discover how to open myself to be available to that power.

The power that is referenced in Step Eleven is a different kind of power than I had been accustomed to in my life. I had always associated power with money, prestige, and authority. It was this type of power that I had wanted in my life. Shortly after getting sober and working with people in recovery, I came to understand that this type of power would not keep me sober, nor would it bring me the happiness in my life that I was seeking. When I was first introduced to this step, it was somewhat frightening, because I associated it with religion. At the time, I was still confused and not ready to engage in any religious activity. I was also not able to spend time alone in any type of quiet setting. I was extremely uncomfortable with silence and was simply not ready for this type of spiritual experience. Yet the program provided me with alternatives to carry me through to the time when I would be able to be intentional in my pursuit of Step Eleven.

My early sobriety consisted of simple prayer and meditation. I came to understand the purpose of these disciplines as a way to communicate with the God of my understanding. I learned that prayer was me speaking to my God, and meditation was me trying to listen. I was able to pray when asking for help to stay away from one drink for one day in the morning when I started my day with prayer. I was also able to say thank you at night for a day of sobriety. From there, I branched out into finding a wonderful book with prepared prayers and meditations each day throughout one year. This small book did not overwhelm me. It provided a brief prayer and meditation for the day, along with a thought for the day. After reading it and offering the suggested prayer, I was able to go about my day with these thoughts rambling around in my brain and popping in and out of my consciousness. It was a wonderful and simple way for me to connect with my God. I did not feel threatened by this process, and it started to teach me about prayer and meditation. It also helped me to continue to grow in my trust with this newfound way of life. It basically felt good, so I continued with it.

Over the years, I acquired a desire to have God included in more than just my sobriety. Today I know that He was involved in every minute of my life and that it was a matter of my recognizing and accepting this reality. However, as I continued to grow with the steps, I started to think about Step Eleven. I was changing, and I now wanted to do God's will in my life. I came to understand if this loving Power was able to keep me sober, than why not try to include Him in other areas of my life. I knew that His will included my living a sober and productive life, trusting in His direction, and surrounding myself with healthy relationships. So I started to think more about this step and how I might become more structured with my prayer and meditation.

My great ambitions collided with an obstacle almost immediately. The obstacle was that no matter how much I tried to incorporate this discipline into my life, I always seemed to fail. I was very busy living life, and it was becoming more and more difficult for me to set aside time for prayer and meditation. I had come to a beautiful understanding of the nature of my God, and called Him by a name that was comfortable for me.

> Those who pray do more for the world than those who fight; and if the world goes from bad to worse, it is because there are more battles than prayer.
> ~George S. Patton, *said prior to the Battle of the Bulge*

I knew that He was kind and gracious, loving and compassionate. Why would

I not want to spend time in conversation with Him? Why could I not maintain this type of discipline? It didn't make sense to me, and I felt like a complete failure. This dilemma haunted me for years.

Finally, I had moved along with a pursuit for additional education, and during one of my courses, I was introduced to the concept of the Myers-Briggs Personality Indicator®, or MBTI. The MBTI is based on the theories of psychologist Carl Jung, and identifies sixteen different personality types. After identifying my personality type, I came to understand that people function differently in this world as a result of their individual human natures. The different personality types operate and respond to life in somewhat predictable ways. The key concept that I learned is that I respond to social situations, decisions, and relationships in a way that is comfortable for my personality. I am different from some people and similar to others. The bottom line was very clear once again: I could not compare myself to others in order to determine whether or not I was okay. I must identify how I function best, accept that this is important information to know about myself, and then adjust my life to my own nature.

When considering prayer and meditation, I came to understand that I am not at my best when I try to schedule a time each day to sit in a quiet space for prayer and meditation. This is absolutely the best approach for many of my friends, but not for me. I am best when I am doing something active and bringing God along with me. I try to exercise early in the morning and use some of this time for my "talking and listening" to God. I live by the water and find it very comforting to walk along the sea wall and see the beauty of this world that I am blessed to live in. I also benefit from a structured church worship service and I find solace in learning new ideas about God's will in my life through the wisdom of those who are preaching. I also have this same experience when listening to a group of recovering alcoholics share their stories and their experience with the Twelve Steps.

The other important aspect of this step in my life is asking for God's power to help me carry out his will for me. The power is there each and every day, and I can witness that when I look at a life of continuous sobriety for well over three decades. So I now ask for this same power to help me in other areas of my life. I have always believed that I was to write a book one day, and when I came to understand that this was the first book I would write, I began to ask for God's power to help me carry this out. I have sought His power in all areas of my life: marriage, parenting, employment, and ministry. I have also learned that it is a little scary in attempting to understand which direction to take when confronted with a major life decision. I truly believe that God honors my best intentions and understands that I will not always be able to discern His will for me. I know today that He will always bless my intentions and efforts, and that I will not be alone.

When it comes to praying for discernment for myself or for special requests for others, I have learned that there is a great ending that I can add to any of my prayers. The *Twelve and Twelve* states that we can end all prayer requests with "Thy will be done."[13] This gives me the comfort of believing that I am not approaching my request as a child would approach Santa Claus, but to know that I am asking for God's power to be used for the best, as He sees it.

Another important concept that I have discovered is that there is no way that I will ever be able to know what God's will for me is if I make my own decisions without consulting Him first. If I choose to say, "Thy will be done" and want to be sincere in this request, then I need to be open to all possibilities of what that decision or direction might be. Otherwise what I am really asking is for God to bless what I have chosen on my own.

After all of the years of my sobriety, I am still amazed at the power of Step Eleven. The power lies not only in finding a way to communicate with God, but also in finding the comfort and serenity of knowing that I am not alone in making my way through my sobriety and my life.

STEP ELEVEN FOR EVERYONE

One of the greatest benefits of incorporating Step Eleven into our lives is the increased awareness of God's presence. This is achieved through both prayer and meditation. The prayers that we use do not have to be our own. There are many different prayers that have been captured throughout the ages that can be used to aid us in this discipline. There are also excellent resources in the form of daily meditation books. These are numerous and can be found in any bookstore or online through various book distributors.

It is best to experiment with a discipline that will be something that is pleasing to do. We are sure to fail at this practice if we try to engage in something that does not fit our personality. But it should also be noted that Step Eleven requires discipline. It can be helpful to initiate this discipline by setting aside an appointment for yourself each day at the same time. For some, the first thing in the morning is desirable and, by getting up early, we can make it part of a regular morning routine. For others, it works at the end of the day and offers a way to focus on Step Ten and Eleven during the same time period.

In *Praying for Wholeness and Healing*, Richard J. Beckmen writes, "Prayerfulness is the state of consciously walking with God through life. Prayerfulness is not so much the act of saying prayers, although that is part of it, as it is living in the awareness of God's presence. This is the goal toward which most serious Christians strive. Yet being prayerful is one of the most difficult disciplines for the Christian to maintain."

THE MYSTERY REVEALED IN THE SIMPLICITY OF STEP ELEVEN

> **We can find power even though we are powerless.**

The mystery in Step Eleven is that by surrendering ourselves to our powerlessness over our addictions, or life in general, we will be available to receive the power that can lead us to a new and amazing life.

STEP ELEVEN

SELF-STUDY QUESTIONS

1. Do you have a way that you pray and meditate on a daily basis? If so, describe what you do and the kind of results that you find from this discipline. If not, what plan will you use to begin this practice?

2. List the words from two of your favorite prayers from the ages. Why are these meaningful to you? What do the words suggest to you?

3. Describe a time in your life when you sought God's will and had to step out in faith to pursue it. What was the outcome?

4. When have you experienced God's power working in your life, other than in helping you to deal with your addictive behavior?

Chapter 12

AWAKENING SPIRITUALLY

STEP TWELVE

HAVING HAD A SPIRITUAL AWAKENING AS A RESULT OF THESE STEPS, WE CARRIED THE MESSAGE TO ALCOHLICS, AND PRACTICED THESE PRINCIPLES IN ALL OF OUR AFFAIRS

Step Twelve is what I call my "automatic step." My own experience and the experience of others suggests that for anyone who has an addiction to alcohol and is serious about working the first eleven steps of Alcoholics Anonymous, this step is automatic. What I mean by this is that it is impossible to avoid a spiritual awakening, it is impossible to avoid sharing this good news with other suffering alcoholics, and it is impossible to not want to follow the principles of this program and to continue with this newfound way of life. These benefits of the program are "automatic" for those who are persistent, rigorous, and honest in working the first eleven steps to the best of their abilities. Step Twelve was automatic for me; I could not avoid it, and I certainly did not want to avoid it. I embraced this step with gratitude and excitement.

The first part of the step states clearly that we will have a spiritual awakening as a result of working these steps. My understanding of the disease of alcoholism was confirmed through my own experience by the time I had completed the first eleven steps of this program and started building my life around it. I experienced significant recovery—physically and mentally—within my first year. I felt better physically than I had since I had started drinking. My mental recovery was also progressing nicely. The fears that had consumed me were reduced to a more manageable level. I was able to drive over bridges and stay in my home by myself without fear. By the time I had established my relationship with God, taken inventory of myself, and made my amends, I was beginning to recognize that my spirit was coming alive in a way I had never experienced in my life.

The literature said that we would experience the "joy of living." I had no concept of joy prior to my recovery from my disease. I had confused happiness and joy by thinking that they were one and the same. They are not. Happiness occurs on a physical and mental level. I am happy when I am with my family and friends. I am happy when I am playing golf on a sunny and warm day in New Hampshire. I am happy when I am productive in my work. Happiness is often a response to people, places, and things in my life. Happiness was the elusive state of mind that I was seeking with alcohol.

Joy, though, is experienced internally and is not dependent upon outside circumstances. Joy emanates from our spirits. Joy and serenity can only come when we are in right relationship with God, ourselves, and others. It was impossible for me to experience true joy until I had engaged in a path of recovery from the disease that had robbed me of my own self-worth and self-esteem.

My spirit was awakened; it came alive when I started to shed the damaged parts of my life—my self-destructive behavior and the baggage that had buried my spirit with shame and guilt. I cannot trace this awakening to any certain date and time. It was a gradual process that grew and strengthened as I matured in my sobriety—one day at a time, as a result of perseverance and honesty. It happened without any fanfare and with little attention on my part. I came to recognize that it had happened when I attended groups that were discussing the Twelve Steps and sharing their own spiritual awakenings. Basically, I came to realize that I felt alive and my spirit was soaring with hope for my life.

My decision to work the steps of Alcoholics Anonymous was based on wanting to stay sober. I did not believe that I would change, and I certainly did not believe that joy was possible for me to experience. I had merely hoped that I would be freed from the bondage of drinking alcoholically. I first noticed the phenomenon of joy in my life when I started to reach out to other alcoholics. When I first got sober, I had the classic reaction of a newly sober person. I wanted to tell all of my friends who drank like I did that they were alcoholics and needed to work this program of recovery. Fortunately, I had learned from others that this would not be a wise course of action! The most powerful message for me to carry to these people would be for them to see me sober and to watch my life change for the better. I am grateful that this was one suggestion I took to heart and followed.

There were certainly a lot of people in my life in 1976 that I wanted to declare as alcoholics and tell them to join me in this pursuit of a new way of life. Many people have passed through my life since those days whom I have also thought had a problem with alcohol and who could benefit from this program. But I learned that this is a disease that can only be diagnosed by the individual who has the disease. Others can tell people that they are alcoholic or have a problem with drinking—a person's physician, clergy, or a judge in a court of law. But even these reputable professionals will most likely deliver this news to deaf ears because of the denial aspect of the disease. So the intent of this part of the step is to not go out into the world and recruit suffering alcoholics and bring them to these steps.

The intent of the second part of Step Twelve—"we carried the message to alcoholics"—is meant for those in recovery to be available to others who seek recovery. It is not meant to be an evangelism step. With that said, the primary intent is for people in recovery to be able to take others to meetings of Alcoholics Anonymous and to share their experience and wisdom with those who want to stay sober. This may appear to be a selfless act of generosity, but the reality is that when we are able to reach out and give of ourselves to another person, the result is the opposite of what we expect. It is amazing to discover the truth in the age-old adage of "you have to give something away to keep it." This was a concept that was totally foreign to me. I had never truly given away part of myself with no expectation of something in return. When I started to share my own experience of recovery, I started to have a glimpse of the joy that this step refers to. Not only did I have the satisfaction of seeing lives changing and people staying sober, I also had an amazing feeling well up inside of me that I came to understand as joy. I began to sense that joy was not about me—joy was about giving myself to others and receiving a payback that was indescribable. I was generous in sharing my time and telling my story of recovery to those seeking sobriety. But I received just as much as I gave away. Some of these people were able to receive the precious gift of sobriety—and I received the priceless and precious gift of joy.

The beauty of this step is that it is indeed selfless and generous.

At this point, I was compelled to continue to share my experience with others—not because of what I would receive in return, but truly because of what I was privileged to witness in their lives. I was able to see changes in others that I had not been able to see in my own life, although I was told that my changes were obvious to those who had helped me. It was remarkable and miraculous to be part of recovery in someone's life. It was humbling, and it was inspiring. I came to understand that I was a vessel of God's grace and that He was able to work through me when I made myself available.

I also came to understand that all people who sought sobriety would not be successful for many different reasons. Some came because they were told to come, and they were not seeking help for their disease. They were seeking to quell the storms around them. I needed to learn that it was not my responsibility to "heal" them; it was only my responsibility to carry the message of hope and to share my own experience. I did not have the power to cure anyone or give them a desire to stay sober. I could not tell them that they were or were not alcoholics. I could only share that no one ever came to Alcoholics Anonymous because they were social drinkers. People came because they were like me. They came because they had a problem with alcohol and needed help. Some stayed, and some did not stay. Those who stayed and became engaged with the steps with sincerity were able to stay sober one day at a time. The truth of this part of the step was that, regardless of the outcome of my "carrying the message," I stayed sober. Each time I shared my story or my experience with the steps, I was reminded of the true nature of my disease and the results of my efforts at working these steps. My own strength and recovery deepened as I received this incredible joy of living.

The last part of Step Twelve was also automatic for me in many ways. Once I had worked the steps and was able to learn how to apply the principles of the steps to my daily living, I was convinced that this was the way of life I wanted to live. There was never a question in my mind that these principles were the core of my ability to stay sober. But the drive to live by these principles went beyond the recovery aspect of the steps.

It felt good to live in this world by a set of principles that were based on truth, honesty, and integrity. I also discovered very early that I was not the sole benefactor of my efforts at working these steps. Each and every person in my life benefited from my new way of life. My family relationships were deepened, my friendships blossomed, and my professional life was enriched. Why would I ever choose to live any other way? It was once and for all the life that I had always wanted. It was a way of life that sustained me in adversity and helped me to celebrate in victories. It offered me a relationship with my creator that was lifesaving and life-giving. It gave me the gift of understanding who I am and being happy with the person that I was created to be. I have love, joy, and serenity. I wish for this profound gift of an abundant life for all people.

> Too often we underestimate the power of a touch, a smile, a kind word, a listening ear, and honest compliment, or the smallest act of caring, all of which have the potential to turn a life around.
> ~Leo Buscaglia

STEP TWELVE FOR EVERYONE

A spiritual awakening as referenced in Step Twelve is not the same as a religious conversion experience. It is important to understand the distinction between these two experiences. It is likely that one could have a spiritual awakening as a result of a conversion experience, but it is not necessarily a given. Spiritual awakenings are aspired to through many different religious traditions and faith practices, Step Twelve of Alcoholics Anonymous clearly states that this phenomenon will occur if one pursues the first eleven steps. In this instance, a spiritual awakening comes from establishing a personal relationship with a Power greater than oneself, and typically as a result of being in a right relationship with this Power, as well as ourselves and others. It was manifested for me with a feeling of being truly alive and at peace with the universe!

The same truth that has been repeated in each of these steps is that the power and grace of the steps are not limited to alcoholics in recovery or to other addicted people. The spiritual awakening in Step Twelve is available to anyone who is willing to work the other eleven steps. There is no doubt in my mind that everyone who does truly experience a spiritual awakening will want to shout the good news from the rooftops. They will want to share the news of their discovery and experiences that are uncovered during the process of working the steps. The results of the steps are so amazing that the need to share the experience comes naturally and is hard to contain. It becomes natural to share our stories and the results of the steps with anyone who is willing to listen—especially those people we encounter who might be struggling with problems like ours. It is similar to finding out that someone is giving away something for free, and we just want to call everyone you know to tell them about it. When we share this amazing news with others, we experience the same joy that I described in my recovery.

> I may not have gone where I intended to go, but I think I have ended up where I intended to be.
> ~Douglas Noel Adams

All addictions rob us of the ability to experience joy. This is because all addictions are self-centered. Life is about alcohol for the alcoholic, and all of life revolves around alcohol. It is the same for the drug addict, spending addict, food addict, or workaholic. We are consumed by our addictions, and they dictate how we will live our life and the choices that we make. For others who are not afflicted with an obsessive or compulsive behavior, they too can be totally self-centered if they are not God-centered.

It is only when we find a way of life that includes sharing ourselves with others for their good that we are able to receive the gift of joy in life. Joy does not come from self-centered actions, even when they appear to be for the benefit of others. We can work for charity and still not experience joy if we are doing the work because we think we should, or it makes us look good.

I also came to understand that it is difficult, if not impossible, to feel joy if we have never felt despair. It is almost as if we would not recognize it if we did not truly experience some type of difficulty in our lives. We appreciate sunshine much more when we have come through a long spell of rain, snow, or gray days. We appreciate freedom when we have experienced bondage. We appreciate feeling healthy after we have gone through a serious illness or even a long bout with the flu. And so it is with joy. Kahil Gibran wrote,

> Your joy is your sorrow unmasked . . .
> The deeper that sorrow carves into your being, the more joy you can contain . . .
> I say unto you, they are inseparable.[14]

The following prayer is attributed to St. Theresa. It is a wonderful concluding summary of the spirit and truth of the Twelve Steps of Alcoholics Anonymous:

> May today there be peace within.
> May you trust God that you are exactly where you are meant to be.
> May you not forget the infinite possibilities that are born of faith.
> May you use those gifts that you have received, and pass on the love that has been given to you.
> May you be confident knowing you are a child of God.
> Let this presence settle into your bones, and allow your soul the freedom to sing, dance, praise and love.
> It is there for each and every one of us.

THE MYSTERY REVEALED IN THE SIMPLICITY OF STEP TWELVE

> **You must give it away to keep it.**

The mystery of the twelfth step is simply that you must give it away to keep it. It is only when we give of ourselves and of our experiences in life that we can receive the joy of living. Logic suggests that we gain when we receive. This is true with finances and other physical aspects of our life. But it is not the case in the spiritual realm. This is where the opposite is true.

The Twelve Steps repeatedly turn the logic of the world upside down. Here is a summary of the steps and their mysteries:

1. Admitted we were powerless over alcohol, and our lives had become unmanageable.
   Asking for help is a sign of strength, not of weakness

In Response to the Steps

2. Came to believe that a power greater than ourselves could restore us to sanity.
   We find hope when we find power outside of ourselves

3. Made a decision to turn our will and our lives over to the care of God as we understood him.
   When we surrender, we win!

4. Made a searching and fearless moral inventory of ourselves.
   The freedom in life does not come from burying our past, our fears, or anxieties; rather the freedom comes when we embrace them and deal with them directly.

5. Admitted to God, to ourselves, and to another human being the exact nature of our wrongs.
   We will only be free when we are no longer in bondage to the fear of our secrets being known.

6. Were entirely ready to have God remove all of these defects of character.
   Preparation to have our defects of character removed is a process where we gain something we need, rather than losing something that we thought we wanted.

7. Humbly asked God to remove our shortcomings.
   When we surrender our defects of character, we discover the person we were created to be.

8. Made a list of all persons we had harmed, and became willing to make amends to them all.
   The process for eliminating the list of people we have harmed starts with creating the list.

9. Made direct amends to such people wherever possible, except when to do so would injure them or others.
   It could appear that talking opens old wounds, yet it is only through talking and seeking forgiveness that we find the closure that is needed for healing.

10. Continued to take personal inventory and when we were wrong promptly admitted it.
    It is easier to stay current with making amends than to procrastinate and delay.

11. Sought through prayer and meditation to improve our conscious contact with God as we understood Him, praying only for knowledge of God's will for us and the power to carry that out.
We can find power even though we are powerless.

12. Having had a spiritual awakening as a result of these steps, we carried the message to alcoholics, and practiced these principles in all our affairs.
You must give it away to keep it.

STEP TWELVE

SELF-STUDY QUESTIONS

1. Describe your spiritual awakening.

2. Who are the people who would benefit from hearing your story?

3. Describe your experience, strength, and hope that you have gained from the Twelve Steps.

4. What are the principles that you learned by studying these steps?

Notes

1. Gordon-Conwell Theological Seminary (2006), http://christianity.about.com/gi/dynamic/offsite.htm?zi=1/XJ&sdn=christianity&cdn=religion&tm=46&gps=205_485_1120_604&f=00&tt=11&bt=1&bts=1&zu=http%3A//www.gordonconwell.edu/ockenga/globalchristianity/resources.php.

2. *Alcoholics Anonymous*, 3rd Edition (New York: Alcoholics Anonymous World Services, Inc., 1976) 63.

3. *Twelve Steps and Twelve Traditions,* thirteenth printing (New York: Alcoholics Anonymous World Services, Inc. 1974) 43.

4. *Alcoholics Anonymous*, 4th Edition, 67.

5. *Twelve Steps and Twelve Traditions*, 53.

6. Ibid, 51.

7. Ibid., 66

8. Philip Yancey, *What's So Amazing About Grace?* (Grand Rapids: Zondervan Publishing House, 1997).

9. *Twelve Steps and Twelve Traditions*, 73

10. *Alcoholics Anonymous*, 76.

11. J.A. Jance, *Payment in Kind* (New York: Avon Books, 1991).

12. *Twelve Steps and TwelveTraditions*, 85.

13. *Twelve Steps and Twelve Traditions*, 105.

14. Kahil Gibran, *The Prophet* (New York: Alfred A. Knopf Publisher, 1978) 29-30.